Questions and Answers
INVENTIONS

The **What**, **When**, **Where**, **How** and **Why**
of everything you need to know about inventions

PaRragon

Bath · New York · Singapore · Hong Kong · Cologne · Delhi · Melbourne

Q

I

ers

S

THE LONDON BOROUGH
www.bromley.gov.uk

Please return/renew this item
by the last date shown.
Books may also be renewed by
phone and Internet

Author: Louise Spilsbury
Consultant: Chris Cooper
Editor: Jane Yorke
Design by: Chris Scollen and Macwiz

This edition published by Parragon in 2008

Parragon
Queen Street House
4 Queen Street
Bath BA1 1HE, UK

ISBN 978-1-4075-1896-1

Printed in Indonesia

CONTENTS

What is an invention? 6

WORK........................... 8
Tractors 10
Dairy machines................ 12
Crop watering 14
Farm chemicals................ 16
GM foods 18
Spinning and weaving 20
Factory products.............. 22
Mass production 24

LIVING AND
COMMUNICATING 26
Heating....................... 28
Washing machines............. 30
Cookers and fridges 32
Household gadgets 34
Shopping..................... 36
Printing 38
Telephones 40
Radio 42
Computers.................... 44
Cameras 46
Cinema 48
Television 50

TRANSPORT, BUILDINGS
AND POWER 52
Cars.......................... 54
Trains 56
Ships 58
Aeroplanes 60
Bikes 62
Submarines 64
Skyscrapers 66
Bridges 68
Steam power 70
Electricity 72
Nuclear power 74
Natural energy sources 76

SPACE 78
Telescopes 80
Rockets....................... 82
Satellites..................... 84
Spacecraft 86
Space stations 88
Space probes................. 90

INDEX 92

WHAT IS AN INVENTION?

What is an invention?

An invention is a new object, like a spring, or a new material, such as nylon, or a process, like freezing food. When something is discovered it needs an invention to make it useful. People discovered fire over a million years ago when lightning caused natural fires. But they couldn't control fire until they had invented a way of making it by rubbing sticks together or striking flints. Matches weren't invented until AD 577 in China.

BELOW Everything made by people has an inventor, the person who came up with the idea for it in the first place.

catapult

mouse trap

Slinky toy invented in 1945

BELOW The first vacuum cleaners were so big that they were taken door to door for hire.

VACUUM CLEANER

VACUUM
II, RUE S.ᵗ F LORENTIN, II
CLEANER

Why do people invent things?

People usually invent things to make life easier. Household appliances, such as the vacuum cleaner, have revolutionized housework. Most inventions develop from earlier ideas. For example, in 250 BC, a Greek inventor called Archimedes explained how levers worked. This led to many other inventions including the scissors, nutcrackers and tweezers. Sometimes, a new invention is an improvement on an old one, such as the vacuum cleaner. But some inventions are made by accident. The Slinky toy was developed when some springs fell off a work bench. Silly Putty was invented while someone was trying to make a material to replace rubber. And Teflon, the non-stick coating used on saucepans, was the result of a mistake by its inventor, scientist Roy Plunkett.

When were most inventions made?

People have always had great ideas but haven't always had the materials or technology to make them happen. In the last 250 years the discovery of electricity, new chemical materials and advances in microbiology have led to an explosion of inventions. Today large companies, universities and governments have research laboratories to develop new inventions.

ABOVE Albert Einstein didn't invent anything, but made many major scientific discoveries that led to countless modern inventions, such as nuclear energy, lasers and microchips.

RIGHT Leonardo da Vinci drew up plans for a submarine in the 15th century, 400 years before the first submarine went to war.

What is a patent?

A patent is a way for inventors to protect their ideas. When an inventor has a new idea, the government can grant a patent to the inventor. The patent gives the inventor the legal right, for a fixed period of time, to stop other people from making, using or selling the invention except with the inventor's permission. Many more inventions are patented than ever succeed. Trademarks also protect the name of an invention. Trademarks tell us the source of a product or service and give us information about quality and consistency. Trademarks have been found on pottery made in around 5000 BC.

RIGHT Inventor Dean Kamem filed a patent for the Segway Human Transporter in 1999. No one knows whether this invention will become a household name.

WORK

Whether people are at work in a factory or a field, inventions have transformed the way we work. Find out how milking machines work, and what irrigation devices farmers use to water their crops. Discover what GM food means and why we might one day be eating purple carrots. Learn about how soap is made, why factories use conveyor belts and how incredible inventions such as spinning wheels and robots have helped us speed up the way we make things.

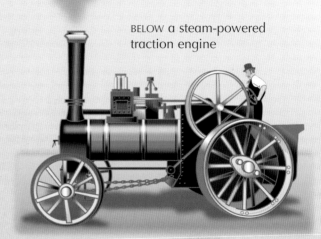

FARMING KEY DATES

| **6000 BC** First stone hand tools for farming | **3500 BC** Ox-drawn plough invented | **2500 BC** Shaduf used to collect water | **260 BC** Archimedean screw used for irrigation | **AD 1810** Metal can invented for preserving food |

TRACTORS

BELOW a steam-powered traction engine

When were tractors invented?

In the 19th century, farmers started to use traction engines to operate farm machines. These heavy engines used steam power to do the work of people or animals. However, early traction engines were expensive to run and too heavy to pull farm machinery over rough or soft ground. In 1892, John Froehlich, from the USA, built the first practical tractor with an engine that ran on petrol.

Large, grooved tyres provide grip on rough ground.

LEFT An open-air tractor harvesting hay.

The three-point hitch is used for attaching farm machinery.

What are tractors used for today?

Today's powerful tractors are comfortable to drive and can pull trailers piled high with heavy loads. They can power different kinds of farm machinery. They drag ploughs to dig fields, giant rakes, called harrows, to break up the soil and seed drills to plant seeds in straight rows. Using a tractor makes farm work quicker and easier for farmers.

Who invented the combine harvester?

In the early 20th century, tractors were often used at harvest time to reap, or cut down, cereal crops such as wheat. Separate threshing machines were needed to separate the grains from the stalks. In 1938, the Canadian company Massey-Harris sold its combine harvester to farmers for the first time. The machine had an engine to power itself along and it could both reap and thresh the crop, so that farmers could harvest larger areas in a faster time.

BELOW The huge cutters on a combine harvester cut down wide strips of crops.

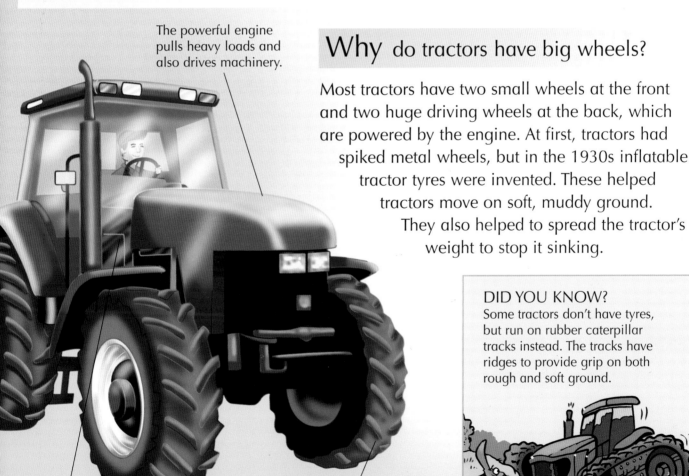

The powerful engine pulls heavy loads and also drives machinery.

Why do tractors have big wheels?

Most tractors have two small wheels at the front and two huge driving wheels at the back, which are powered by the engine. At first, tractors had spiked metal wheels, but in the 1930s inflatable tractor tyres were invented. These helped tractors move on soft, muddy ground. They also helped to spread the tractor's weight to stop it sinking.

DID YOU KNOW?
Some tractors don't have tyres, but run on rubber caterpillar tracks instead. The tracks have ridges to provide grip on both rough and soft ground.

A glass cab allows the farmer to see all around when operating machinery.

The front and back wheels steer separately so that the tractor can turn in very small spaces.

FARMING KEY DATES

| **6000** BC First stone hand tools for farming | **3500** BC Ox-drawn plough invented | **2500** BC Shaduf used to collect water | **260** BC Archimedean screw used for irrigation | AD **1810** Metal can invented for preserving food |

DAIRY MACHINES

When was the milking machine invented?

Milking a herd of cows by hand was a long, hard job before American engineer L.O. Colvin patented his time-saving milking machine in 1860. The farmer attached rubber cups to a cow's teats and then pumped on some bellows. This sucked milk out of the udder through hoses into a bucket. But the machine sucked milk constantly, which often damaged the cow's teats.

How do milking machines work?

Today's dairy farmers use automated milking machines. These can milk a large herd of about 100 cows in a couple of hours. In the milking shed, the farmer first washes the cow's four teats and then attaches the milking cups. The machine's vacuum pump gently sucks the teats in an on-off motion. This draws the milk from the udder in the same way that a calf does.

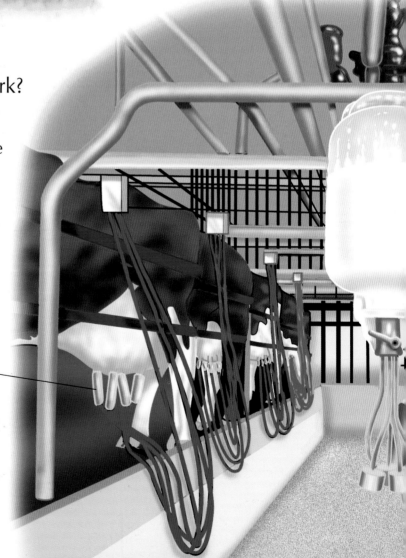

Milking cups are attached to the teats on each cow's udder.

RIGHT The milk from each cow runs along pipes into jars where it is measured. Then the milk is pumped into a large cooling tank. It is stored here until it is collected by tanker and taken to the milk processor.

12

Who invented cheese?

People have been using milk to produce cheese for over 5,000 years. Cheese was probably invented by nomads in the Middle East, who travelled with their goat and sheep herds looking for fresh pasture. The story goes that a nomad once stored milk in a saddlebag made from a sheep's stomach. Warmed by the sun, the milk mixed with the rennet in the animal's stomach and formed curdled lumps – the first cheese.

The curd is chopped and mixed with salt to form cheese.

BELOW When milk is warmed and mixed with rennet it forms lumps of curd and watery whey.

The whey is drained off.

Weigh jars record how much milk each cow produces.

What is pasteurized milk?

Pasteurization is the process of heating food to destroy the harmful bacteria in it and make it safe to eat. The process is named after its inventor, French chemist Louis Pasteur, who first tested it on milk in 1862. Most milk today is pasteurized by being quickly heated to 72° Celsius. This kills any bacteria that are in the milk and helps keep it fresh for longer.

DID YOU KNOW?
Robotic milking sheds allow cows to go in to be milked at any time. Computers trigger the removal of the milking cups when a cow's udders are empty.

FARMING KEY DATES

| 6000 BC
First stone hand
tools for farming | 3500 BC
Ox-drawn plough
invented | 2500 BC
Shaduf used to
collect water | 260 BC
Archimedean screw
used for irrigation | AD 1810
Metal can invented
for preserving food |

CROP WATERING

Why do farmers water their crops?

Plants, like all living things, need water to live and grow. In places with plenty of rain, crops naturally get the water they need. In countries of the world that are drier, or during times of low rainfall, many crops can grow only if they are watered by people. The different methods farmers use to water their crops are called irrigation.

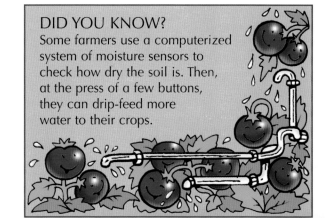

DID YOU KNOW?
Some farmers use a computerized system of moisture sensors to check how dry the soil is. Then, at the press of a few buttons, they can drip-feed more water to their crops.

When was the shaduf invented?

The shaduf is a simple machine invented in Ancient Egypt in around 2500 BC. It is still used to help people collect water from rivers today. The shaduf has a long pole balanced on a pivot. It has a bucket at one end and a heavy rock at the other to act as a counterweight. The bucket is first pulled down into the river and filled with water. Then the load is easily lifted up by the weight of the rock pulling down on the pole.

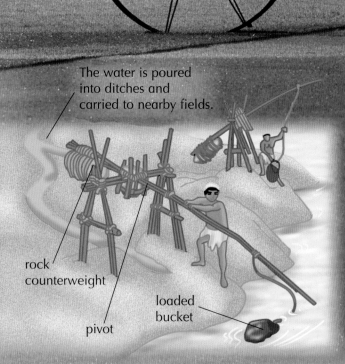

The water is poured into ditches and carried to nearby fields.

rock counterweight

pivot

loaded bucket

How does the Archimedean screw work?

The Archimedean screw is an early type of pump still used in some places to raise water for irrigation. It was first written about by the Greek engineer Archimedes in around 260 BC. The machine has a hollow tube with a tight-fitting screw inside. One end of the machine is dipped in the river and scoops up water as the screw is turned. Water travels to the top of the tube, where it runs out into an irrigation ditch.

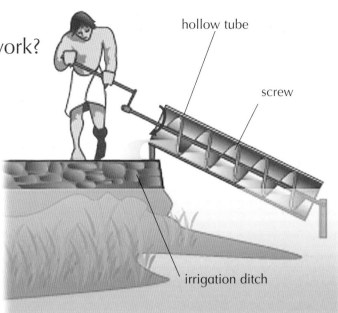

hollow tube

screw

irrigation ditch

What do modern farmers use for irrigation?

Today, many farmers use a system of electric pumps, pipes and sprinklers to move water from rivers and reservoirs to their crops. Pivot irrigation uses motors or water pressure in the pipes to move spray arms in a circle, so that all areas of a field are watered. However, water spray can quickly evaporate from plants in hot sun. Drip irrigation uses holes in pipes, laid on or in the ground, to get water directly to the crop roots.

BELOW A circular field is watered with a long sprinkler arm on wheels, which turns like the hands of a clock.

15

FARMING KEY DATES

6000 BC	3500 BC	2500 BC	260 BC	AD 1810
First stone hand tools for farming	Ox-drawn plough invented	Shaduf used to collect water	Archimedean screw used for irrigation	Metal can invented for preserving food

FARM CHEMICALS

Why do farmers use chemicals?

Many crop farmers use chemical pesticides and fertilizers to help increase the amount of food they can grow. Fertilizers add nutrients to the soil, helping plants to grow bigger and produce more leaves or fruit. Pesticides include insecticides that remove insect pests, herbicides that kill weeds, and fungicides, which are sprayed on crops to prevent plant diseases or moulds.

ABOVE Farmers hire small planes called 'cropdusters' to spray pesticides over large fields. By spraying pesticides from a plane, the operator is safely out of the way of the chemicals.

BELOW Farmers wear protective clothing when spraying herbicides by hand.

What were the first insecticides?

Insecticides are chemical sprays used by farmers to repel or kill the insect pests that eat their crops. People have used natural substances to get rid of insects since ancient times. Some bug-destroyers of the past include salt, tobacco, red pepper and poisonous arsenic. In 1939, Swiss chemist Paul Müller discovered that a chemical called DDT made a good insecticide. Since then a great many chemical insecticides have been produced and sold.

LEFT Some crop pests, such as this blisterbeetle, spoil plants by eating their leaves. Others feed on roots or suck sap from stems.

When are farm chemicals harmful?

In some parts of the world, farmers use huge amounts of chemicals, which is not good for the natural environment. Some of these pesticides and fertilizers harm or even kill plants and harmless animals, such as rare wildflowers or butterflies. When the chemicals wash into the soil and rivers they can pollute them. And chemical traces left on crops, such as lettuce or fruit, can make people sick, if they eat too many of them.

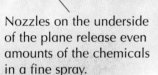

Nozzles on the underside of the plane release even amounts of the chemicals in a fine spray.

DID YOU KNOW?
As long ago as 4500 BC, farmers in Mesopotamia burnt sulphur from nearby volcanoes. The stinky smoke kept insect pests off their crops.

How do organic farmers grow crops?

BELOW Farmers check their fields throughout the growing season for signs of pest damage.

Organic farmers grow crops without using artificial chemicals. They use compost and manure from farm animals in place of artificial fertilizers. These farmers also encourage wildflowers to grow in their herbicide-free fields. Some flowers attract helpful insects, which eat the crop-destroying bugs. Organic farmers can also deter insect pests by growing smelly plants, like garlic, or spraying natural insecticides like the bitter-tasting oil from the tropical neem tree.

17

FARMING KEY DATES

| 6000 BC First stone hand tools for farming | 3500 BC Ox-drawn plough invented | 2500 BC Shaduf used to collect water | 260 BC Archimedean screw used for irrigation | AD 1810 Metal can invented for preserving food |

GM FOODS

What is GM food?

GM stands for 'genetically modified'. GM food comes from plants or animals that have had their genes altered by scientists. Genes are the inherited chemical 'instructions' found in all living cells that make plants and animals the way they are. Scientists can now alter food plants by removing or adding extra genes to create new crops that stay fresh longer, are not spoilt by pesticides, or can grow in dry soils.

LEFT GM peaches are disease-resistant.

> **DID YOU KNOW?**
> GM scientists have created purple carrots and orange cauliflowers that contain around 25 times more vitamins than the usual kinds. These vegetables would certainly make dinnertime more colourful!

BELOW Some GM sunflowers produce a healthier type of oil.

When were GM foods invented?

The first GM food plant went on sale in 1994. The 'Flavr Savr' tomato contained an altered gene to keep it firm and fresh for longer. Most tomatoes are picked when green and ripened later. The modified tomatoes were picked when red and did not go soft during transportation. They tasted better than ordinary tomatoes because they were ripened on the plant.

How are plants genetically modified?

Scientists can shoot new genes directly into plant cells using a special kind of gun. Next, the cells are put into a liquid, which helps them grow into whole plants. Scientists can also add new genes to bacteria, which then infect plant cells and modify its genes. This is how a frost-resistant gene from a fish was put into a tomato plant. The result was tomato fruits that are not damaged by cold weather.

LEFT Scientists monitor their GM experiments by growing modified plants in greenhouses.

GM protesters worry that GM crops are not safe in the environment. They fear that GM crops might cross-breed with normal crops growing in nearby fields.

BELOW GM wheat is not damaged by herbicides.

Who knows if GM crops are safe to eat?

Some people are concerned that genetic modification could be harmful to human health. They say that scientists don't fully understand how genes work and that altering plant genes could create foods that are poisonous or cause allergies. GM scientists and supporters say that no one eating GM foods has yet become sick and GM crops are needed to help farmers grow enough food to feed all the people on Earth.

MANUFACTURING KEY DATES

5000 BC	AD 1000	1733	1764	1771
Loom invented for weaving cloth	Spinning wheels used to make yarn	Flying shuttle first used for weaving	Spinning jenny invented	First factory with powered machines

SPINNING AND WEAVING

DID YOU KNOW?
The American Eli Whitney had the idea for a cotton-cleaning machine in 1793, after seeing a cat use its claws. His invention, called a gin, had rows of sharp hooks which separated cotton fibres from their sticky seeds.

Who invented the spinning wheel?

Spinning wheels are machines that help to make strong thread or yarn. They were invented by textile workers making cloth in Asia, in around AD 1000. The operator spins a large wheel on a frame. This pulls and twists together short fibres of cotton or wool into long continuous yarn, which is wound onto a spindle. In 1764, the Englishman James Hargreaves invented the spinning jenny machine that could wind thread onto many spindles at a time.

thread winds onto the spindles

RIGHT Hargreaves' spinning jenny

cotton fibres

When was the loom invented?

The handloom was invented in around 5000 BC for weaving fabrics or carpets from yarn. One set of yarns, called the warp, are tied vertically to the wooden loom. Then another set of yarns, called the weft, are woven in and out across the warp to make cloth. In 1733, the Englishman John Kay invented the flying shuttle. This was a spindle with weft yarns wrapped around it that could be quickly knocked back and forth across the loom. It made weaving much quicker.

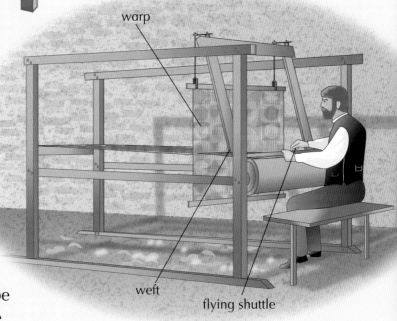

warp

weft

flying shuttle

ABOVE Kay's flying shuttle loom

What did the first factory produce?

In the earliest factories, textile workers made cloth completely by hand. The world's first factory with powered machinery was built by the Englishman Richard Arkwright in 1771. His cotton mill in Cromford employed lots of workers. They operated spinning machines, invented by Arkwright, and looms to weave cotton cloth. The machines were first powered by water wheels and later by steam engines. Arkwright built houses nearby for his mill workers to live in.

BELOW Cromford mill was built beside a river and used the water to power its spinning and weaving machines.

How do industrial looms work?

The industrial looms of today are huge, computerized machines and are housed in vast factory warehouses. They operate without flying shuttles. Now, jets of high-pressure air or water are used to shoot weft yarns at speed between the warp. Each loom is programmed to select different yarn colours and create complex patterns in the cloth it weaves. One textile worker can look after 20 looms at the same time.

LEFT Traditional industrial looms are still used in small factories today.

BELOW Colourful spools of yarn used for weaving.

MANUFACTURING KEY DATES

5000 BC	AD 1000	1733	1764	1771
Loom invented for weaving cloth	Spinning wheels used to make yarn	Flying shuttle first used for weaving	Spinning jenny invented	First factory with powered machines

FACTORY PRODUCTS

BELOW Baekeland named his discovery Bakelite. This hard plastic was used to make many everyday objects, like this telephone.

When was plastic invented?

In the late 1800s, natural materials such as bone, shell and ivory were used to make buttons, knife handles and other products. These were expensive, so inventors created a new material, called celluloid, in 1863. This artificial material was produced by adding chemicals to cotton fibres and was the first type of plastic. In 1909, a chemist from New York, USA, invented the first true plastic made just from chemicals. Leo Baekeland discovered that his sticky mixture could be moulded into shapes and baked hard.

LEFT Celluloid was used to make objects that looked like ivory or bone, such as this baby's hairbrush.

What is plastic used for today?

Plastic has quickly become the major industrial material because it is waterproof, easily moulded into shapes, and cheap to produce. Different plastics can be soft or hard, flexible or stiff, coloured or transparent depending on the chemical ingredients used to make them.

Factory-made plastic objects are all around us, from the insides of cars and fridges to toys, clothing, CDs and mobile phones.

BELOW In the past, outdoor toys, like this tricycle, were made of heavy, sharp metal that rusted easily. Today's trikes are built from hard-wearing, colourful plastic.

RIGHT Many liquid products, such as washing detergent, are packaged in plastic bottles. These have replaced heavy, glass bottles that could smash if dropped.

Why is aluminium recycled in factories?

Since 1958, aluminium has been used to make cans for drinks. Aluminium is a light metal that can be extracted from rocks and clays. But many new cans are actually made from old ones. At a recycling plant, waste cans are melted down and poured into moulds to form metal ingots. The ingots are taken to a factory where huge rollers press them into thin sheets of aluminium. Machines cut the sheets into pieces and join them together to produce new cans ready for filling.

DID YOU KNOW?

People throw away millions of plastic bottles each day, but they are put to good use if recycled. They are shredded and turned into polyester fibres to make new carpets, clothing or more bottles.

How is soap made?

Bars of soap are made by heating plant oils or animal fats together with an alkali, such as wood ash. This produces soap and a substance called glycerine. In a factory, the glycerine is removed, and the soap is dried before perfumes and colourings are added. The soap is then cut into pieces, pressed into shape and wrapped into the bars we buy in the shops.

LEFT A lot of clothing is now designed to keep you warm, to be long-lasting, waterproof or fast-drying, thanks to new fabrics made with plastic fibres.

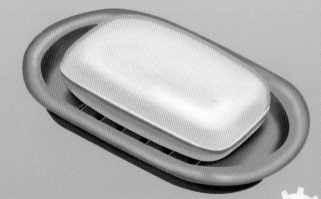

23

5000 BC Loom invented for weaving cloth	AD 1000 Spinning wheels used to make yarn	1733 Flying shuttle first used for weaving	1764 Spinning jenny invented	1771 First factory with powered machines

MASS PRODUCTION

BELOW Brunel's factory produced 130,000 pulley blocks a year.

Where did mass production begin?

In the first factories, one worker would often make a whole product from start to finish. Then in England in 1802, French-born engineer Marc Isambard Brunel began mass-producing wooden pulley blocks for ships' rigging. His factory used 45 different steam-driven machines. To speed up production, each worker had a single job to do to each pulley block before passing it on to the next worker.

Who created moving assembly lines?

Ransom E. Olds created the first moving assembly line in his American motor car factory in 1901. He started using conveyor belts to speed up his car production process. The conveyor belts carried the cars to workers in different parts of the factory. Workers quickly added the same part to every passing car. The faster production times meant that assembly-line cars could be sold more cheaply.

RIGHT Olds' assembly line was copied by other early car manufacturers, such as Henry Ford in the USA.

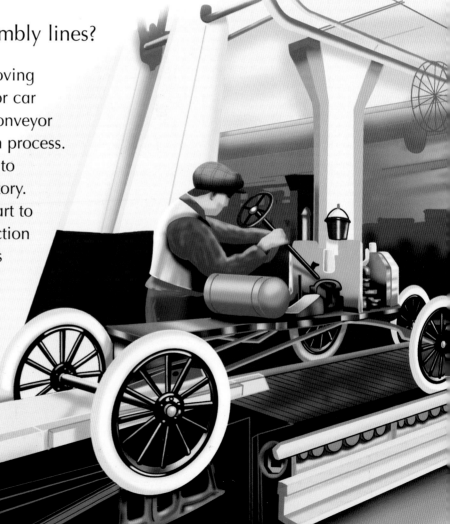

When were industrial robots invented?

One problem with assembly lines is that workers can get bored repeating the same job, and tired machine operators can make mistakes. A solution was found in 1961, when an industrial robot was installed in an American car factory for the first time. Programmed by computer, the robot carried out the dangerous job of unloading and stacking hot metal parts from a machine.

DID YOU KNOW?
Sensors in computer-controlled robotic arms make sure that they repeat exactly the same movements again and again – without ever getting weary!

RIGHT Industrial robots are quick and accurate. They perform many manufacturing tasks, such as welding, painting, assembling parts and testing finished products.

A robotic arm has moving joints powered by motors.

Early cars were put together quickly on a conveyor belt.

What is mass customization?

Mass customization is when goods are made to suit a customer's needs using mass production processes. Modern computer technology makes it possible for factories to build the basic components of a product, such as a car, and then put together a specially made version. For instance, customers might order a specific paint colour for their car, a personalized computer, or a CD with their own selection of songs.

LIVING AND COMMUNICATING

Inventions play a vital role in how we live, relax and communicate in our everyday lives. Find out how a fridge-freezer works and how melting chocolate led to the invention of the microwave oven. Discover the inventions that have changed the way we shop, when the first books were printed and who invented the typewriter. Learn how computers have shrunk from the size of a room to fit on a lap, how radios can carry voices over the globe and what the first words ever to be spoken over a telephone were.

DAILY LIFE KEY DATES

400 BC	100 BC	AD 800	1596	1893
Romans build central heating hypocaust	First coins made in China	Chinese invent paper money	Flushing toilet invented	Zip invented to replace bootlaces

HEATING

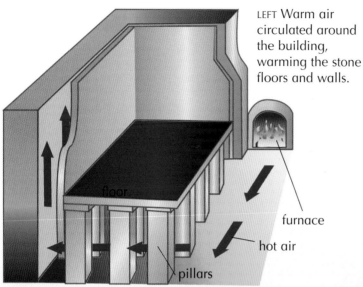

LEFT Warm air circulated around the building, warming the stone floors and walls.

floor

furnace

hot air

pillars

Who invented central heating?

Keeping homes warm has always been a challenge in cold places or during winter. The Ancient Romans invented the first central heating system, called a hypocaust, in 400 BC. A fire in a room against an outside wall fed heated air under the house. The floors were raised on pillars and the walls were hollow so the heat flowed around the whole building warming the stone walls and floors.

Where were gas fires invented?

The first really successful gas fires for the home were invented in England by engineer Sigismund Leoni in 1881. A gas valve or tap is turned to release gas from a pipe and the gas is lit. Heat comes from the gently burning gas, but many fires also have fake coals or rocks that glow red hot.

DID YOU KNOW?
In Iceland, water heated by hot rocks underground comes to the surface in springs. This is collected and piped to homes for heating and for hot tap water!

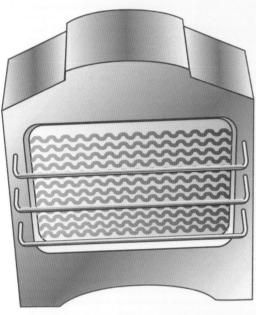

ABOVE An electric current passing through a coiled filament heats it up, warming the air around it.

When was the electric fire invented?

The method for making an electric fire came from several sources, but the first household electric fire was patented in 1892 by Bell Crompton and his partner, Herbert Dowsing, in the UK. In an electric fire, electricity passes through a heating element. The heating element converts electrical energy into heat energy and, as it gets hotter and hotter, some of this heat escapes into the air and warms up the room.

How do radiators work?

In modern central heating systems hot water is pumped through metal radiators. Heat from the radiator warms the air that flows past it. This warm air rises and colder air flows in to take its place. This circulation develops a flow of air around the room, sending warm air away from the radiator and delivering cooler air back to be heated.

RIGHT This type of convection radiator was invented by Franz SanGalli in 1855.

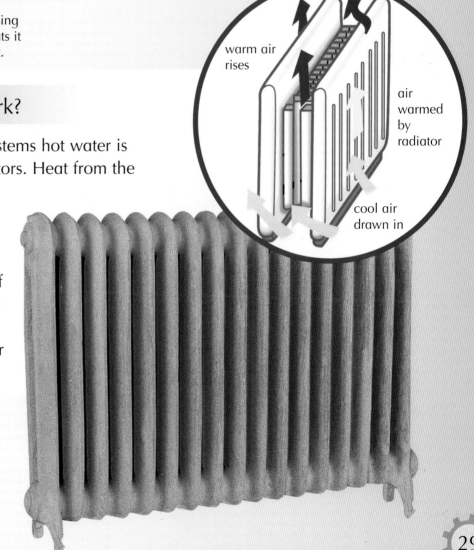

warm air rises

air warmed by radiator

cool air drawn in

29

DAILY LIFE KEY DATES

400 BC	**100** BC	AD **800**	**1596**	**1893**
Romans build central heating hypocaust	First coins made in China	Chinese invent paper money	Flushing toilet invented	Zip invented to replace bootlaces

WASHING MACHINES

Where was the washing machine invented?

The very first washing machine was made in America in 1874. It consisted of a wooden tub with small wooden pegs inside that you turned with a handle. Soapy clothes were tumbled about to get clean. The first electric washing machine with a rotating drum was invented in 1907 by Alva J. Fisher in the USA. By the 1960s, fully automatic washing machines were available that could wash, rinse and spin at the touch of a button.

BELOW Laundry goes into a drum at the front with a watertight seal around the door.

Wet clothes were lifted out and fed through the wringer to squeeze out the water.

Wooden pegs inside the tub rotated the laundry.

ABOVE The washtub was filled by hand with hot soapy water.

How does a washing machine work?

Most washing machines work by tumbling dirty laundry, soap and water around inside a moving drum to loosen the dirt. Then the drum spins round very fast so that the soapy water comes out of the laundry, drains through the little holes in the drum and flows away. You just have to press a button to program the washing machine's computer to tell it how strong or long each wash needs to be.

soap drawer

spinning drum

Draining holes allow water to flow in and out.

A heavy weight keeps the machine in place while it is spinning.

When was the first dishwasher invented?

The first dishwashers, which appeared in the USA around 1900, were turned by hand. Unfortunately, these took a long time to wash a few dishes, leaked a lot and often didn't work properly. Americans had to wait until the 1940s for the first boxed-in electric dishwasher that also rinsed dishes. They were not available in Europe until 1960.

DID YOU KNOW?
Early washing machines helped clean clothes but washing was made easier still in 1861 when the wringer was invented to get the water out of laundry after washing.

RIGHT Dishwashers clean by spraying hot water and detergent onto dirty dishes. Then clean water rinses away the soapy water.

Why was soap invented?

Water has surface tension and doesn't wash things well, so people invented soap. People began to make soap from about 2800 BC. The soap was made by boiling fat with wood ash, and was used to wash clothes. The first artificial laundry soaps, called detergents, were invented in the 1920s when American chemists created chemicals that loosen dirt from laundry in water, so that the dirt is washed away.

DAILY LIFE KEY DATES

| 400 BC
Romans build central
heating hypocaust | 100 BC
First coins made in
China | AD 800
Chinese invent
paper money | 1596
Flushing toilet
invented | 1893
Zip invented to
replace bootlaces |

COOKERS AND FRIDGES

gas burner

gas tap

gas oven

ABOVE The first gas stoves were made from heavy cast iron.

Who invented the first cooker?

The first gas cooker was invented by James Sharp in England in 1826. The first electric stove was invented in the USA by William Hadaway in 1896. Gas cookers use flames to heat pans of food, while electric hobs have a coil of wires that heat up when high current electricity flows through them.

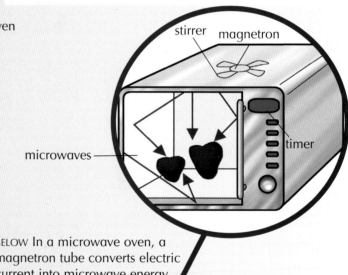

stirrer   magnetron

microwaves

timer

BELOW In a microwave oven, a magnetron tube converts electric current into microwave energy. A 'stirrer' rotates to make sure the microwaves don't concentrate in one place.

Who invented the microwave oven?

American researcher Percy Spencer discovered microwaves when he paused in front of some radar equipment and realized the chocolate in his pocket was melting! The chocolate was being cooked by invisible electromagnetic waves called microwaves. The company he worked for sold the first microwave oven in 1945. When something is hot, it's because its molecules are vibrating quickly. Microwaves make water molecules in food vibrate quickly and this cooks the food.

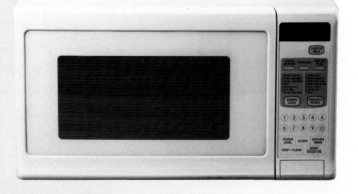

When was the refrigerator invented?

The first refrigerators were invented in England in the 19th century. These were simple wooden boxes lined with metal and an insulating material, such as cork, which held blocks of ice to keep food cool. The first fridges as we know them appeared in 1914. By the 1920s, the first electric refrigerators with freezer compartments were sold.

DID YOU KNOW?
For hundreds of years people cooked over open fires, but in 1490 the first oven – a brick box that trapped heat from a fire – was invented in France.

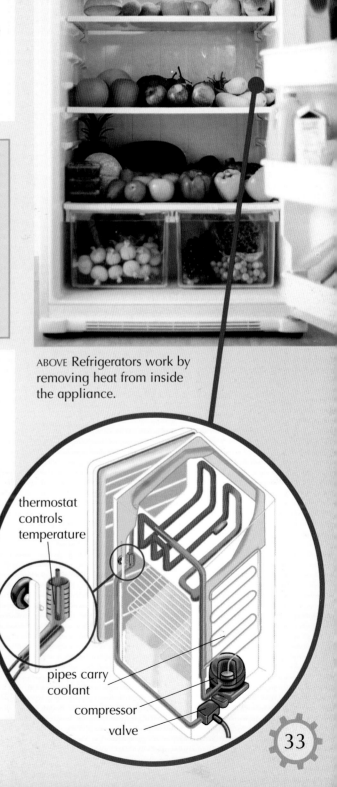

ABOVE Refrigerators work by removing heat from inside the appliance.

thermostat controls temperature

pipes carry coolant

compressor

valve

How do fridge-freezers work?

Fridges and freezers work using a special substance called a coolant. The coolant, in the form of a gas, goes through a compressor where it turns into a liquid. Compressing the coolant makes it warm. The warm liquid passes through zig-zag pipes on the outside of the fridge and cools down to room temperature. The coolant is forced through a valve under pressure, and expands suddenly, turning into gas and cooling. The cold gas circulates in pipes inside the fridge-freezer, cooling the air and so keeping the food and drinks cool. The gas gets warmer and passes through the compressor to start the cycle again.

DAILY LIFE KEY DATES

400 BC	100 BC	AD 800	1596	1893
Romans build central heating hypocaust	First coins made in China	Chinese invent paper money	Flushing toilet invented	Zip invented to replace bootlaces

HOUSEHOLD GADGETS

BELOW The first irons got their name because they were made of the metal iron. They were heated directly over a gas flame or hot oven plate.

Who introduced the electric iron?

American Henry W. Seely introduced the electric iron in 1882 and it was one of the first gadgets made to use electricity. The hot plate of an iron is warmed by a heating element inside. The heat is controlled by a thermostat that switches the electric current on and off to keep it at the right temperature.

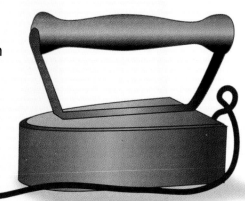

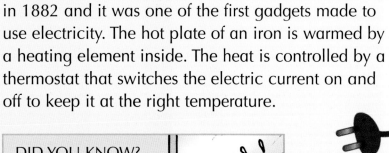

DID YOU KNOW?
The first pop-up toaster was invented in the USA in the 1930s, but the country's economy was in a depression so few people could afford the luxury of buying one!

When were vacuum cleaners invented?

In 1901, English engineer Cecil Booth came up with the idea of a device to remove dust using suction. He tested the idea by sucking in a handkerchief over a dusty chair and saw that the dust collected on the handkerchief. He patented the first vacuum cleaner, the Puffing Billy, later that year, using a petrol-burning internal-combustion engine to power the suction. It was so big it had to be pulled from house to house by a horse-drawn cart.

BELOW Today's vacuum cleaners have a small electrical motor. This turns a fan inside, pulling air and dirt in through a filter that collects the dirt in a bag or chamber that can be emptied.

1901
Horse-drawn vacuum
cleaner in service

1945
Microwave ovens on
sale for first time

1970
First bar code used on
chewing gum

1982
Smart card invented for
public telephone calls

How do hairdryers work?

The first hand-held hairdryers were invented in 1920 in the USA and although the outer designs have changed, the insides basically work in the same way today. Hairdryers have metal wires inside that get hot when electricity flows through them. The hot wires heat air as it is blown past them and out through the hairdryer nozzle by a motor-operated fan. The warm air dries your hair by evaporating the water away.

fan

heated
filaments

electric
motor

nozzle.

switch

Where were food processors invented?

The first food processor was invented in France in 1971 and it was called a Magimix. Food processors save cooks time and energy because they can mix dough and chop, slice, dice and even liquidize different foods. To make them work, food processors have motors inside that convert electrical energy into spinning movement energy to turn blades and other tools inside a bowl.

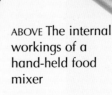

ABOVE The internal
workings of a
hand-held food
mixer

35

DAILY LIFE KEY DATES

400 BC	100 BC	AD 800	1596	1893
Romans build central heating hypocaust	First coins made in China	Chinese invent paper money	Flushing toilet invented	Zip invented to replace bootlaces

SHOPPING

BELOW Harrods, one of the world's most famous department stores, lit up for Christmas.

When were shops invented?

The first shops were invented in 650 BC in Turkey, in the same area that silver coins were first used. These were permanent places where goods were bought and sold. Before that, people traded from temporary market stalls. In the 1700s, stores with separate departments that sold different goods first appeared. These were the first department stores.

DID YOU KNOW?
The first self-service supermarkets with car parks appeared in the USA in the 1930s.

RIGHT James Ritty's first cash register.

Who invented the cash register?

The first mechanical cash register was invented in 1879 by an American called James Ritty to stop his staff stealing change. By pressing keys, the machine added up how much money was spent and showed it on a dial that he could see. Today, most cash registers scan bar codes and people no longer have to tap in numbers.

1901
Horse-drawn vacuum
cleaner in service

1945
Microwave ovens on
sale for first time

1970
First bar code used on
chewing gum

1982
Smart card invented for
public telephone calls

How do bar codes work?

Bar codes are striped black and white labels that save time at checkouts. A laser on a bar code reader shines a beam of light that bounces off the bar code. The cash register then automatically identifies what the item is and adds its price to your bill. The first product to have a bar code was a packet of Wrigley's Gum in the 1970s.

ABOVE The bar code reader recognizes the unique pattern of stripes on each item in the shop.

BELOW Online shopping is quick and easy.

What is Internet shopping?

Shopping on the Internet is just like ordering something over the telephone, except you use a computer to do it. You usually pay for an item by credit card and stores deliver the goods to your home. The first Internet shopping site was Amazon.com, which began selling books in 1995. American computer scientist Jeff Bezos is said to have started the business from his garage.

37

COMMUNICATIONS KEY DATES

| AD 150 | AD 500 | 1450 | 1660 | 1844 |
| Paper first invented | Quill pens used with ink | First printing press | First postal service introduced | Electric telegraph in use |

PRINTING

Why was the printing press invented?

The earliest books were rare and expensive because they were written out by hand. The invention of the printing press meant many copies of a book could be printed quickly, so that more people could read it. The German goldsmith Johann Gutenberg perfected the first printing press in 1450. He made raised metal letters on blocks, called type. These were arranged as words in lines to form each page. Black ink was rolled onto the type and the letters were pressed onto paper to copy each page.

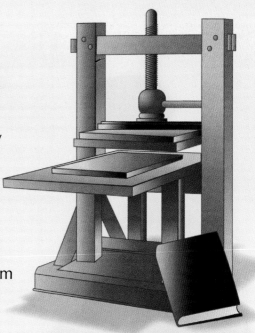

ABOVE It took two or three people to produce one page using Gutenberg's printing press.

DID YOU KNOW?
The earliest books were printed in China in around AD 868. Words and pictures were carved into wooden blocks. These were then inked and pressed onto paper.

BELOW A typewriter from the early 1900s

ink ribbon

Who invented the typewriter?

The first successful typewriter, invented by the American Christopher Sholes was put on sale in 1874. His writing machine enabled fast typists to make neat printed pages of text without jamming the keys. The design slowed typists down slightly by placing the common letter keys in positions that are harder to hit.

The QUERTYUIOP arrangement of letter keys designed by Sholes is still used on computer keyboards today.

How are pages printed today?

Today, the colour pages of books and magazines are usually printed on offset printing presses. Computer software is used to convert designed pages into flat metal printing plates. There are separate plates for four basic coloured inks – cyan, magenta, yellow and black – and each one is wrapped around a cylinder. One ink colour is rolled onto the plate as the cylinder rotates. Water is also rolled onto the plate to keep the non-printing areas ink-free. The plate then transfers the inked page onto a soft, rubber roller, which prints the words and pictures onto a roll of paper. Once the paper dries, it is overprinted in the same way with the inks on the other three colour plates.

water rollers
ink rollers
impression cylinder
plate cylinder
offset rubber cylinder
paper

ABOVE Automated, offset printing presses are very fast and accurate.

ABOVE Laser printers are widely used to print personal documents.

What is desk-top publishing?

Desk-top publishing started in 1985, when people were first able to use page design software on their personal computers. They could create their own documents and print them inexpensively on a laser printer. Desk-top publishing software enables anyone to design pages with different styles of type and headings and include pictures such as photographs and graphics. Once the laser printer receives the image data from the computer, it can quickly and quietly print multiple copies of the finished colour pages.

COMMUNICATIONS KEY DATES

AD 150	AD 500	1450	1660	1844
Paper first	Quill pens used	First printing	First postal service	Electric telegraph
invented	with ink	press	introduced	in use

TELEPHONES

What was the electric telegraph?

The electric telegraph was first used in 1844 to send a message between the American cities of Washington and Baltimore. This communications system transmitted the letters of the alphabet using a code of dots and dashes. It was invented by the Americans Samuel Morse, Joseph Henry and Alfred Vail. A 'Morse code' message was sent down a cable from one telegraph station to another by tapping a key. This switched the electric power supply on and off. A receiver at the other end recorded the signals as dots and dashes. The code was then translated back into words.

> DID YOU KNOW?
> Videophones were first made in the 1990s to let callers see the person they are talking to. A small video camera records the caller's face. The pictures are sent down the phone line to the videophone's TV screen.

RIGHT A telegraph key was used to tap out Morse code messages.

BELOW Early telephones had no dials or keys for putting in phone numbers. All calls were connected by an operator.

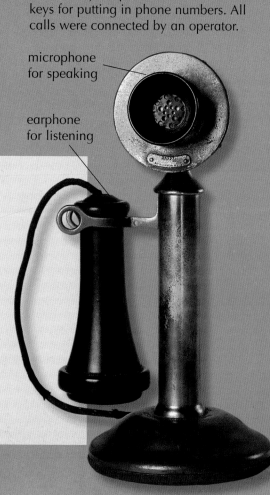

microphone for speaking

earphone for listening

Who invented the telephone?

In 1875, the Scottish inventor Alexander Graham Bell became the first person to transmit the human voice along an electrical wire. Bell had been looking for a way of sending several telegraph messages at once down a wire, when he accidentally spilled acid on his clothes. As Bell cried for help, his assistant heard his words, 'Mr Watson! Come here, I want you!' coming from the machine they had built. This surprise discovery led to his invention of the telephone in 1876.

How do modern telephones work?

When a phone number is tapped into the keys of a telephone, it sends a series of electrical signals along the telephone network to an exchange. Here powerful computers route the call to the correct destination. Seconds later, the receiving phone rings as the call is connected. Telephones also change the callers' voices into electrical signals. These either travel along copper cables, or are changed into pulses of light and sent along optical fibres made of thin strands of glass. International calls are sent via satellite links, which transmit the signals as radio waves.

BELOW The telephone network

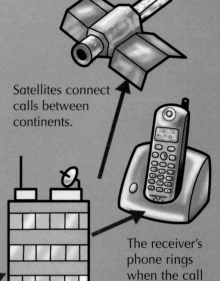

Satellites connect calls between continents.

The caller's phone dials a number.

The local exchange connects local numbers or routes the call to a national exchange.

The national exchange forwards the call.

The receiver's phone rings when the call is connected.

The mobile phone exchange connects calls to cell phones.

When were mobile phones invented?

The first cell, or mobile, phone was developed in 1973 by the American Martin Cooper. Early mobile phones were known as car phones, as they were designed for use in a car. Today's mobile phones allow people to make and receive calls from almost anywhere. They work by sending and receiving calls using invisible radio-wave signals. These travel through the air to a nearby mobile phone exchange, which connects the call through to the right number.

RIGHT Your mobile phone information is stored on a SIM card (Subscriber Identity Module).

COMMUNICATIONS KEY DATES

AD 150	AD 500	1450	1660	1844
Paper first invented	Quill pens used with ink	First printing press	First postal service introduced	Electric telegraph in use

RADIO

Who invented radio?

The Italian electrical engineer, Guglielmo Marconi, combined the ideas of other inventors to build the first successful radio transmitter in 1896. It used electric sparks to create radio waves that were picked up by a receiver over six kilometres (four miles) away. Radio transmitters work by turning sound into electrical signals, which are in turn changed into radio waves. Invisible radio waves can travel long distances through the air at the speed of light.

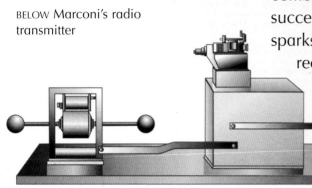

BELOW Marconi's radio transmitter

What was the first radio broadcast?

The earliest radio transmissions were messages sent in Morse code, often for the military. In 1906, the first sound radio broadcast was made in the USA by the Canadian inventor, Reginald Fessenden. He used his transmitter to broadcast music and a reading from the Bible to the public. However, Fessenden's audience was small, as home radio receivers were not available for sale until the 1920s.

BELOW Early radio receivers, like this one, were called a 'wireless' because they picked up signals without needing telegraph cables.

DID YOU KNOW?
The British inventor, Trevor Baylis, built the world's first successful clockwork radio in 1991. The radio is powered by winding a handle, which charges the batteries inside.

When were the first transistor radios?

The first small, portable radios went on sale in 1954, thanks to the invention of the transistor. Tiny transistors were able to make sound signals louder and quickly replaced the large glass valves of early radios. Transistor radios could also work with small batteries as the electric circuit needed less power.

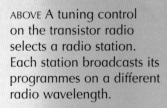

Radio signals are made louder by a transistor.

Battery power makes radios light and portable.

ABOVE A tuning control on the transistor radio selects a radio station. Each station broadcasts its programmes on a different radio wavelength.

BELOW Digital radios have a small screen that can display information about the programme on air.

Radio waves broadcast from a transmitter are picked up by an aerial.

Why was digital radio invented?

Digital radio broadcasts first began in 1995 to provide listeners with a wider choice of programmes, better sound quality and more programme information. The latest digital radios let listeners pause, rewind and record live programmes. Digital radio works by turning sound and text data into digital signals. The signals are transmitted as radio waves and picked up by digital radio receivers. These have the software to decode and turn the signals back into sound and text.

43

COMMUNICATIONS KEY DATES

AD 150	AD 500	1450	1660	1844
Paper first invented	Quill pens used with ink	First printing press	First postal service introduced	Electric telegraph in use

COMPUTERS

ABOVE The world's first successful electronic computer, called ENIAC, was used to make scientific calculations for the US army.

Who invented the computer?

The English mathematician Charles Babbage invented a steam-powered mechanical computer in 1822. However, neither the technology nor funding existed at that time to build his calculating machine. In 1946, the first fully programmable electronic computer was built by John Eckert and John Mauchly in the USA. This enormous, automatic calculating machine filled a room in the University of Pennsylvania.

DID YOU KNOW?
The fastest, most powerful, computers in the world are called supercomputers. In just one second, they can make calculations that a calculator would take 10 years to do.

When was the first PC built?

The first personal computers, or PCs for short, were developed in the 1970s. The Americans Steve Jobs and Steve Wozniak invented the first successful PC for home use in 1977. Their electronic *Apple II* computer had a colour screen and keyboard built into one box. Today's PCs can be programmed to do a vast number of different jobs, from word processing and working out calculations to operating computer games.

BELOW *Apple II* personal computer

The computer disk drives are used to input programs or store data information.

keyboard

colour screen

1876
First telephone invented

1896
First radio transmitter

1938
Ballpoint pen developed

1977
First personal computer

1981
Internet opened to the public

BELOW The hard-disk unit houses the important electronic components that run the computer, including the disk drives, CPU and RAM.

a CPU computer chip

RAM memory

How do computers work?

Electronic computers work at high speed processing data in the form of text, numbers, pictures or sounds. They complete their tasks by following the instructions of software programs, which can be loaded onto the machine. The heart of a computer is the hard-disk unit. This contains the central processing unit, or CPU, which controls all of the operations of the PC. The CPU is a microprocessor – a small chip of silicon containing several electronic circuits. The data is stored and retrieved using memory chips called RAM.

What are laptops?

Laptops are small, portable, battery-powered computers. They were invented in 1982 so that business people could use their computers away from the office, for example, travelling on a train, or working from home. Laptops have the same parts and capabilities as PCs, but they are usually small enough to fit in a briefcase. They have a folding case with a built-in keyboard and screen. A touch-pad controls the cursor, instead of an external mouse.

RIGHT Laptop computers are small and light enough to carry anywhere.

touch pad

ENTERTAINMENT KEY DATES

| 4000 BC
Board game
Senet invented | 1000 BC
Yo-yos popular in
Greece | AD 1700
First piano
constructed | 1827
First photograph is
taken | 1878
Edison's phonograph
plays recorded sound |

CAMERAS

ABOVE A plate camera

Who took the first photo?

Frenchman Joseph Niépce took the first photograph in 1827. He fixed a metal plate coated with light-sensitive chemicals inside a box that let in no light except through a lens at the front. Eight hours later, an image of the view from the room's window had appeared on the plate. Niépce and others developed plates that took quicker photos.

DID YOU KNOW?
The 'camera obscura', invented in 16th century Italy, was a darkened room with a small hole that projected the scenery outside onto a wall.

When was the first roll of film invented?

In 1888, the American George Eastman made a camera that took photos on a roll of paper film. Using roll film meant that people could take several photos without having to change plates after each one. It also meant that cameras could be smaller. In 1900, Eastman's Kodak company started to sell the first popular small camera, the box Brownie, for $1.

RIGHT Kodak's motto was 'You push the button and we do the rest.'

film

press to take a photo

camera settings

What is an SLR camera?

Invented in 1935, the SLR camera lets photographers see through the lens to accurately know what their photo will look like. In other film cameras, the view through the viewfinder is slightly different to that through the lens. When you take a photo using an SLR, a mirror flips up to let light from the lens hit the film rather than go into the viewfinder.

BELOW A CMOS image-sensing microchip turns light into electrical signals in a digital camera.

Pushing a button opens a small window, called the shutter, for a split second to let light hit the film.

Twisting the lens focuses to make sure you get a clear picture. Some SLR cameras have automatic focus.

Inside an SLR camera

CMOS

How does a digital camera work?

Digital cameras, invented in 1988, have a light sensor instead of film. The sensor is a screen divided into tiny squares called pixels. Pixels measure the different colours of light making up an image and a computer chip converts this into a sequence of numbers. Images are stored in memory space inside a camera and also on removable memory cards.

ENTERTAINMENT KEY DATES

4000 BC	1000 BC	AD 1700	1827	1878
Board game Senet invented	Yo-yos popular in Greece	First piano constructed	First photograph is taken	Edison's phonograph plays recorded sound

CINEMA

Who invented cinema?

Most people agree that Auguste and Louis Lumière of Lyon, France, invented cinema. In December 1895, they showed moving pictures of factory workers to an audience. The Lumière brothers invented the cinematographe which took lots of photos in a sequence on a long roll of celluloid film. They projected the film onto a wall by shining light through it as they wound the film.

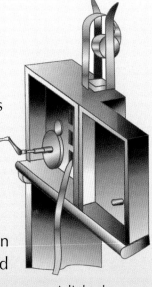

ABOVE A light shone through the images as they passed the lens.

DID YOU KNOW?
Toy Story, released in 1995, was the first full-length computer animated movie ever. Special computer graphic (picture) programs produced most of the images of toy cowboy Woody and spaceman Buzz Lightyear.

When were sound movies first made?

The first short sound movies were made in 1923 by Phonofilm. A new process could record sound onto a strip along the edge of film so the sound and image were always synchronized together. Before then, the only sound in cinemas was from musicians, such as piano players, who played along with a film in the movie house. *The Jazz Singer* of 1927 was the first successful talkie, or film with speaking actors.

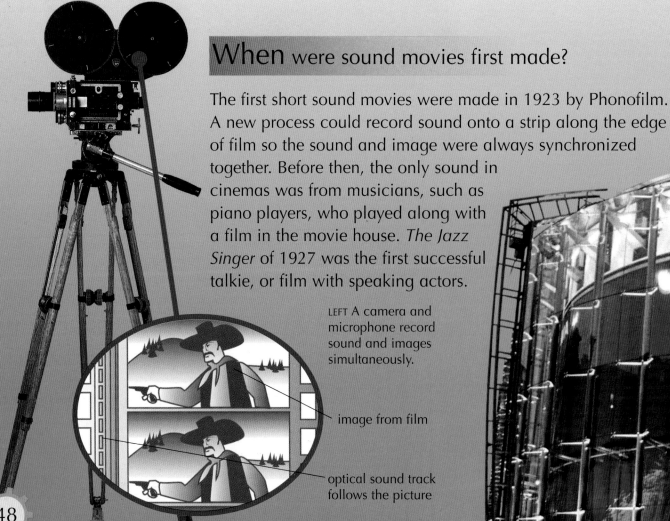

LEFT A camera and microphone record sound and images simultaneously.

image from film

optical sound track follows the picture

How do moving pictures work?

Moving pictures work because of a trick of the eye. Each image or frame in a film sequence shows the same objects in slightly different positions. When the sequence is played fast enough, the objects appear to move. The film is fed through a projector which shines a light through the film and projects it onto a white surface where the image appears larger.

A light beam is projected.

LEFT Film runs through the projector where a light shines the image through a lens.

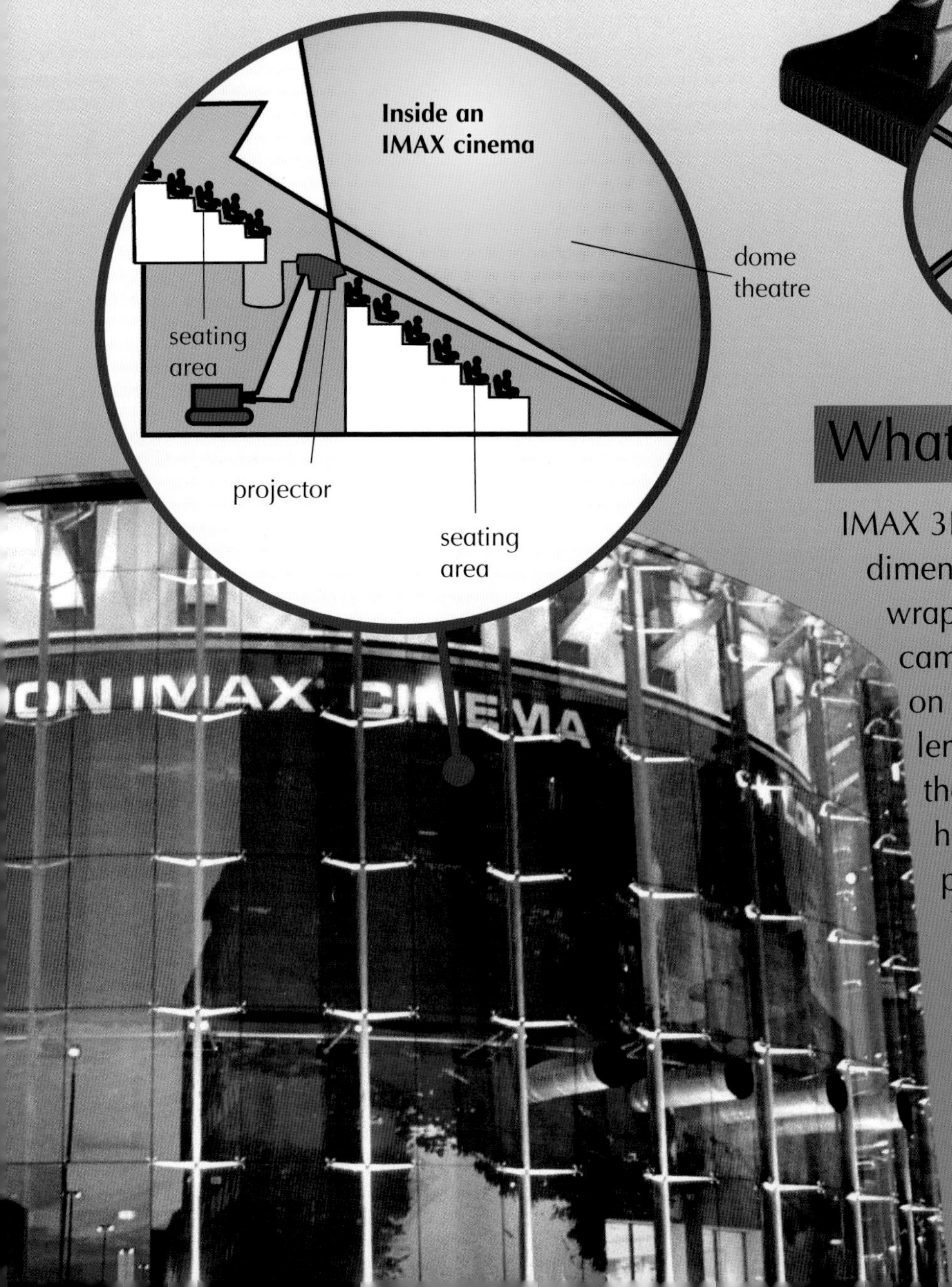

Inside an IMAX cinema

seating area

projector

seating area

dome theatre

What is an IMAX 3D cinema?

IMAX 3D cinemas show 3D (three-dimensional) films on enormous, wrap-around screens. IMAX cameras record the same scene on two rolls of film through two lenses 64mm apart (2½ inches), the average distance between human eyes. The two rolls are projected at the same time. Viewers wear special glasses to make sure that each eye sees the correct image for that eye.

LEFT The Imax Cinema in London has a cinema screen the height of five double-decker buses.

ENTERTAINMENT KEY DATES

4000 BC	1000 BC	AD 1700	1827	1878
Board game Senet invented	Yo-yos popular in Greece	First piano constructed	First photograph is taken	Edison's phonograph plays recorded sound

TELEVISION

Who invented television?

In 1925 Scottish inventor John Logie Baird transmitted the first recognizable television image. Unfortunately, his mechanical television gave people headaches. Russian-born engineer Isaac Shoenberg came up with a better electronic system in 1936. But it was fellow Russian Vladimir Zworykin who added a cathode ray tube to create as well as display pictures.

LEFT Logie Baird's first television.

Where were the first television broadcasts made?

The BBC started regular broadcasts of TV programmes in 1936 from London, England. TV cameras converted each second of movement and sound into electrical signals. Aerial transmitters made the signals stronger so they could travel long distances through the air. TV aerials detected the signals and the cathode ray tube converted them into moving pictures on TV screens.

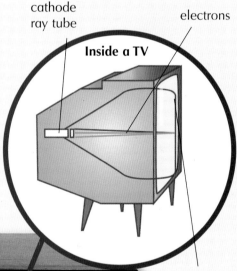

cathode ray tube

electrons

Inside a TV

phosphor-coated screen

ABOVE In the cathode ray tube, beams of electrons strike phosphors which coat the inside of the screen. The phosphors glow to make the picture.

ABOVE Television programme being broadcast from a studio in the 1960s.

ABOVE TV pictures were in black and white until the 1960s.

1895
Lumière brothers
show the first film

1902
Teddy Bear named
after Roosevelt

1925
Logie Baird invents
television

1962
First satellite TV
broadcast

1989
Game Boy
invented

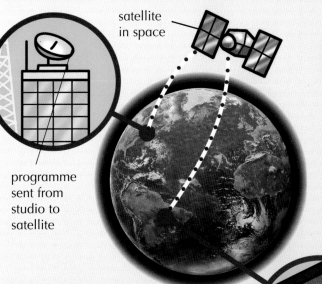

satellite
in space

programme
sent from
studio to
satellite

satellite dish
on your house
receives the
images from the
satellite

When was satellite TV first broadcast?

The first satellite TV broadcast in July 1962 used communications satellite Telstar 1 to send images of the American flag across the Atlantic Ocean. For satellite TV, a transmitter on Earth broadcasts signals into space. The satellite bounces back scattered signals to different parts of the Earth, where they are collected using satellite dishes connected to TVs.

A digibox
converts
signals
arriving via
cable or
satellite into
a TV picture.

What is digital television?

Digital TV uses digital signals that often produce sharper pictures and better sound than traditional analogue signals. Digital signals can carry many more channels, as well as extras such as programme information. Programmes can be interactive, for example viewers can take part in quizzes, or pay for extra programmes using the TV.

DID YOU KNOW?
The biggest flat panel TVs are far lighter than cathode ray tubes and so thin they can be mounted on the wall like a picture.

A remote
control uses
an infra-red
beam to
change the
TV settings.

51

TRANSPORT, BUILDINGS AND POWER

Since ancient times, people have found ingenious ways to transport themselves, create structures to live and work in, and power their daily lives. Learn about crucial transport inventions, from sailing ships to modern jet planes. Find out what the world's tallest building is. Discover how a steam engine works and find out about the natural energy sources that will power our future.

TRANSPORT KEY DATES

| **7000 BC** First dugout canoes and rafts | **3500 BC** First sailing boats and wheeled carts | **AD 400** Catamaran boat invented | **1783** First hot-air balloon flight | **1825** First steam railway in use |

CARS

RIGHT Karl Benz's first motor car had only three wheels.

internal combustion engine

When was the car invented?

German engineer Karl Benz invented the first petrol-driven motor car in 1885. By using the earlier invention of the internal combustion engine (invented 1859), Benz was able to build a practical motorized vehicle. However, his car travelled very slowly and passengers sat up high and in the open. Early cars were expensive and it wasn't until 1910, when Henry Ford began making cheaper mass-produced cars in the USA, that more people could afford to drive.

Why do car engines need petrol?

Modern cars have an internal combustion engine. The engine burns petrol or diesel inside a cylinder to produce the energy to propel the car along. The burning fuel drives a piston up and down, which powers the driveshaft. This then turns the wheel axles to make the car move. A battery provides electricity for the starter motor and spark plugs, which together start the engine.

The driver uses pedals and other controls to speed up or brake the car and to change gear.

ABOVE Drivers refuel their cars at a petrol station. The petrol is pumped through a hose with a nozzle into the fuel tank.

RIGHT There are usually four cylinders in a car engine. Inside each one, the spark plug ignites a mixture of fuel and air, which explodes and pushes the piston down.

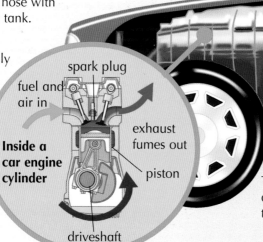

spark plug

fuel and air in

Inside a car engine cylinder

exhaust fumes out

piston

driveshaft

The gearbox changes the amount of power going to the car's wheels.

The driveshaft connects the gearbox to the rear axle.

1870
Penny farthing
bicycle invented

1885
First petrol-driven
motor car

1903
First successful
aeroplane flight

1939
Modern-style
helicopter invented

1976
First supersonic
passenger plane

HOW fast can racing cars go?

On the straight stretch of a race track, purpose-built racing cars can zoom along at 300 kilometres (186 miles) per hour. Racing cars reach these high speeds because their engines are more powerful and work faster than those in normal vehicles. Racing cars are also built low to the ground and specially shaped to reduce air resistance.

ABOVE The chequered flag marks the finish line.

DID YOU KNOW?
The world's cleanest cars are air-powered. Their piston engines run on compressed air, which is stored in tanks underneath the vehicle.

driver's cockpit

Wide rubber tyres grip the road.

The front and rear wings on this Indy car help to keep the vehicle pressed to the road at high speeds.

fuel tank

The exhaust pipe releases waste gases from the engine.

What are battery-powered cars?

Battery-powered cars are electric vehicles that run on batteries. Their invention came about because of people's concerns about pollution caused by petrol exhaust fumes. However, electric car batteries are big and heavy. They can store only enough power for a vehicle to travel a certain distance before they need to be plugged into a mains electricity supply and recharged.

TRANSPORT KEY DATES

| 7000 BC First dugout canoes and rafts | 3500 BC First sailing boats and wheeled carts | AD 400 Catamaran boat invented | 1783 First hot-air balloon flight | 1825 First steam railway in use |

TRAINS

When was the first passenger steam railway?

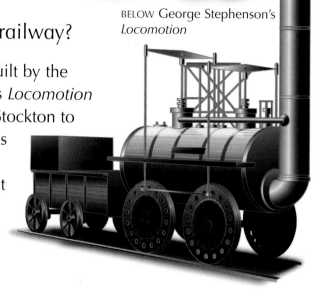

BELOW George Stephenson's *Locomotion*

One of the first passenger steam railways was built by the British engineer George Stephenson in 1825. His *Locomotion* engine pulled open passenger carriages on the Stockton to Darlington Railway in England. Its top speed was just 25 kilometres (15 miles) per hour. This was much quicker than earlier railways, where freight wagons were pulled along iron rails by horses.

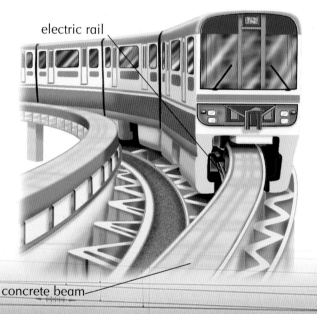

electric rail

concrete beam

How do monorail trains work?

Monorail trains run above or hang below a single rail or track. The earliest monorail was built in 1880. Today, most monorail trains run on wheels along the top of the concrete beam that forms the track. Guide wheels also run along the side of the beam and help to keep the train steady. Electric rails provide power and some trains operate without drivers.

What are maglev trains?

Maglev trains have no engines or wheels. They levitate, or float, just above a track. Maglev is short for 'magnetic levitation'. A powerful magnetic field is created by coils of electrically charged wire in the track. This works with strong magnets on the train to lift it up and propel it forwards. Maglevs go faster than other trains because they are not slowed down by the friction caused by wheels on tracks.

ABOVE Maglevs can travel at an amazing speed of 500 kilometres (310 miles) per hour.

RIGHT A TGV train

The pantograph draws electrical power from an overhead wire above the track.

Where do TGV trains operate?

The streamlined TGV is France's *Train à Grande Vitesse*, which means high-speed train. These electric passenger trains run on special tracks and can travel as fast as 300 kilometres (186 miles) per hour, making them the fastest conventional trains in the world. Most high-speed trains today are pulled by powerful electric or diesel engines.

The TGV's on-board computer in the driver's cab controls all the train's working systems.

Electric motors power the engine's driving wheels.

DID YOU KNOW?
The world's first underground railway was opened in London, England, in 1863. Passengers travelled on the Metropolitan Line in carriages pulled by steam engines.

TRANSPORT KEY DATES

| 7000 BC | 3500 BC | AD 400 | 1783 | 1825 |
| First dugout canoes and rafts | First sailing boats and wheeled carts | Catamaran boat invented | First hot-air balloon flight | First steam railway in use |

SHIPS

mainsails   mainmast

When were large sailing ships built?

Small boats can travel along rivers and coastlines, but large ships can venture across open oceans. Around 3000 BC, the Egyptians were building large ships with square sails attached to a mast. In the early 1800s, clipper ships with many sails were the fastest cargo ships on the sea. Today, modern tall ships from countries around the world take part in annual sailing races.

RIGHT Modern tall ships are rigged traditionally with square sails attached to the masts.

mizzen sails

BELOW A tourist river steamer today with a paddle at the back.

What are paddle steamers?

The first paddle steamer was built in France in 1783. The ship had a steam engine to drive two four-metre paddle wheels on its sides, which propelled the vessel forwards. Steam ships needed to carry lots of coal to fuel their engines, so ships became much bigger. In 1897, English engineer Charles Parsons tested a new steam turbine engine, which made steam ships much faster than before.

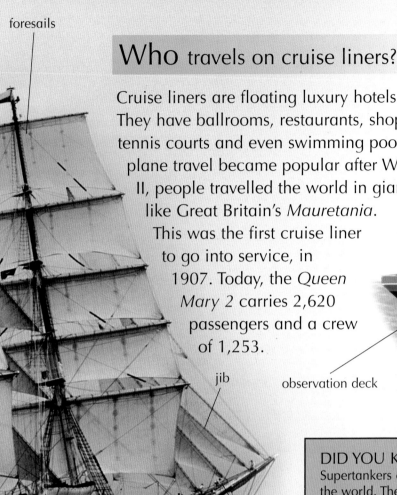

foresails

jib

bowsprit

Who travels on cruise liners?

Cruise liners are floating luxury hotels for tourists. They have ballrooms, restaurants, shops, cinemas, tennis courts and even swimming pools. Before plane travel became popular after World War II, people travelled the world in giant liners like Great Britain's *Mauretania*. This was the first cruise liner to go into service, in 1907. Today, the *Queen Mary 2* carries 2,620 passengers and a crew of 1,253.

observation deck

BELOW The *Queen Mary 2* is the world's largest cruise liner.

passenger cabins

DID YOU KNOW?
Supertankers are the largest ships in the world. They can carry two million barrels of oil. They are so big, it can take them 10 kilometres (6 miles) to stop!

How are passenger ferries powered?

Since 1939, most modern ships, including ferries, have had diesel engines. These turn underwater propellers, which drive the ships through the water. Roll-on–roll-off ferries have built-in ramps, so that cars, trucks and other vehicles can drive on and off easily when the ship is in port. The first such ferry ran in Scotland in 1851. It had railway lines on board, to carry steam trains across a river.

TRANSPORT KEY DATES

7000 BC	3500 BC	AD 400	1783	1825
First dugout canoes and rafts	First sailing boats and wheeled carts	Catamaran boat invented	First hot-air balloon flight	First steam railway in use

AEROPLANES

BELOW The Wright brothers' famous *Flyer* plane of 1903

When was the first plane flight?

In 1903, two American brothers, Wilbur and Orville Wright, built the first powered aeroplane that flew for any distance. Their home-made aircraft had a petrol engine connected to two propellers by bicycle chains. Orville controlled the plane by pulling wires that bent the fabric wings slightly. His historic first flight lasted just 12 seconds and was recorded on camera.

ABOVE Today, the gigantic 555-seat *Airbus A380* is the largest passenger plane in the sky.

How do jet planes work?

The first jet engine was built by the British engineer Frank Whittle in 1937. But Ernst Heinkel built the first jet plane in Germany in 1939. Most airliners today are powered by fanjet engines. These have a large fan that sucks air in at the front. Some of this air is forced into a combustion chamber, where fuel is added and burnt to create hot gases. These drive the fan and blast out of the back of the engine, helping to force the aeroplane forwards. However, most of the thrust, or forwards push of the plane, comes from the air that passes around the engine.

Inside a fan-jet engine

Cool air is sucked in.

Hot air is blasted out.

combustion chamber

Some air passes around the engine, cooling it and providing most of the thrust.

Where do jump jets operate?

Most planes need a long runway to take off. Jump jets can take off with a very short run or even rise straight up into the air. The first vertical take-off plane was the British fighter *Harrier* jump jet, built in 1966. It was designed to operate from an aircraft carrier in the ocean. The plane has four nozzles, which direct the jet engine thrust downwards for vertical lift.

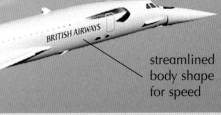

ABOVE Once airborne, a jump jet's nozzles turn so they can propel the plane forwards.

DID YOU KNOW?
The superjumbo *Airbus A380* is so big, its tail is as high as a seven-storey building and there would be room for 70 cars to park on its wings!

ABOVE *Concorde* cruised at around 2,160 kilometres (1,342 miles) per hour – almost twice the speed of sound.

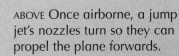

streamlined body shape for speed

What is a supersonic plane?

A plane that flies faster than the speed of sound – 1,225 kilometres (761 miles) per hour – is supersonic. The first plane to break the sound barrier flew in 1947 and in 1976 *Concorde* became the first supersonic jet to operate a passenger service. *Concorde*, designed by British and French engineers, stopped flying passengers in 2003.

TRANSPORT KEY DATES

7000 BC	3500 BC	AD 400	1783	1825
First dugout canoes and rafts	First sailing boats and wheeled carts	Catamaran boat invented	First hot-air balloon flight	First steam railway in use

BIKES

When was the first bicycle made?

The very first bicycle, called the hobby horse, was invented in 1819. It was made of wood, had no pedals, and you pushed it along the ground with your feet. The first bike with pedals to power the back wheels was the *velocipede*, invented in 1839. However, the first bicycle that looked like those we ride today was the *Rover* safety bicycle. It was built in 1885 by the British engineer John Starley. It had a chain, a diamond-shaped frame and equal-sized wheels with spokes.

DID YOU KNOW?
Before 1888, wooden wheels and iron tyres gave cyclists a very bumpy ride. Bicycles today have rubber pneumatic, or air-filled, tyres thanks to Scottish inventor John Dunlop.

RIGHT The *Rover* safety bicycle

What was the penny farthing?

British engineers invented the penny farthing in 1870. This odd bicycle was named after two coins of the time – the large penny and the small farthing – because of the difference in the size of its wheels. Each turn of the pedals made the bicycle travel a long way on the large front wheel. Unfortunately this high-wheeled bike was unsafe to ride and was often in accidents. So when the safety bike was invented in 1885, the penny farthing soon disappeared.

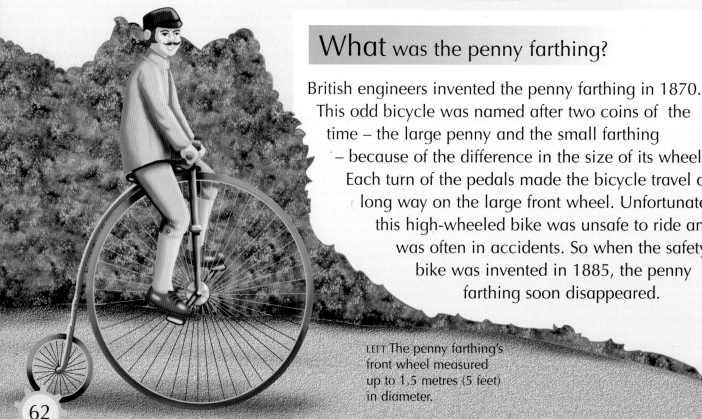

LEFT The penny farthing's front wheel measured up to 1.5 metres (5 feet) in diameter.

BELOW A modern bicycle frame is made from lightweight metal tubing or carbon fibre-reinforced plastic, which is light and strong.

saddle

handlebars

brake cable

gear sprockets

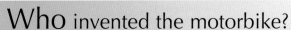

chain   pedal

How do modern bicycles work?

To make a bicycle move, you use your feet to push the pedals, which turn the chain that drives the back wheel round. This makes the whole bike move forwards. To stop the bike, a rider uses the brake levers on the handlebars. These operate cables that pull brake pads against the wheels to slow them down and stop them turning. Gears help riders to cycle uphill in comfort by altering the number of times the rear wheel turns for each turn of the pedals.

Who invented the motorbike?

In 1885, German engineers Gottlieb Daimler and Wilhelm Maybach designed the first two-wheeled motorbike to run on a petrol engine. Today's motorbikes have a steel frame with the engine, gearbox, saddle, fuel tank and other parts attached to it. The engine drives a shaft, or chain, that turns the back wheel. As with a bicycle, it is the back wheel that pushes the motorbike forwards.

RIGHT The police use motorbikes to patrol busy highways.

engine   fuel tank   chain   exhaust

63

TRANSPORT KEY DATES

| 7000 BC | 3500 BC | AD 400 | 1783 | 1825 |
| First dugout canoes and rafts | First sailing boats and wheeled carts | Catamaran boat invented | First hot-air balloon flight | First steam railway in use |

SUBMARINES

When was the submarine invented?

The first submarine was built in 1624 for the English King, James I. This underwater boat, invented by the Dutchman Cornelius Drebbel had a wooden frame covered with a waterproof skin of greased leather. The submarine was powered by 12 oarsmen, who sat inside the leaking vessel and rowed along under the River Thames. Snorkel airtubes, floating on the surface of the water, enabled the submarine to stay under water for several hours.

What are submarines powered by?

The first modern military submarine was powered by a combination of diesel and electric engines. It was developed by the Irish inventor John P. Holland in 1901. Many submarines still work in the same way today. When travelling on the surface, a diesel engine is used to drive the propeller and push the submarine through the water. An electric motor is used for underwater operations. Since 1954, many submarines have run on nuclear-powered engines. These enable submarines to stay hidden underwater for months at a time without refuelling.

RIGHT Submarines are used to seek and destroy ships and other submarines.

DID YOU KNOW?
Small non-military submarines, called submersibles, are used for special underwater tasks, such as exploring shipwrecks or studying ocean life.

A submarine has a streamlined hull to cut through water easily.

64

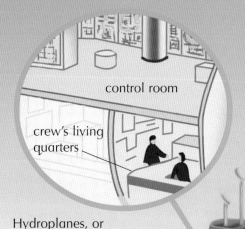

control room

crew's living quarters

The periscope allows the captain to see what is on the surface while the submarine is underwater.

How do submarines work?

Today's submarines have strong steel hulls to withstand high water pressure. A submarine can dive by filling the ballast tanks on either side of its hull with water. This makes the vessel heavier and it sinks. When resurfacing, compressed air is pumped into the tanks to blow the water back out. A submarine has two or three decks divided into many rooms. Sections of the vessel can be closed off in case of leaks in the hull.

Hydroplanes, or fins, tilt for diving and resurfacing.

engine room

propeller

LEFT Torpedoes are launched by compressed air from tubes in the nose and rear of the submarine.

Who invented the torpedo?

The English engineer Robert Whitehead invented the self-propelled torpedo in 1866. These deadly underwater missiles were first used by warships and later carried by military submarines for firing at and sinking enemy ships. Whitehead's weapon had a propeller powered by compressed air to drive it along, and moving fins to steer its path.

The conning tower contains the communication aerials and periscope.

torpedo tube

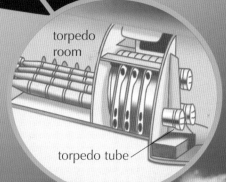

torpedo room

torpedo tube

LEFT Modern torpedoes have sensors and are guided to their targets by signals from the submarine.

65

BUILDING KEY DATES

| 4000 BC
First canals
in use | 3500 BC
First oven-baked
clay bricks | 2000 BC
Clapper bridges
used to cross rivers | 700 BC
First aqueduct built
to carry water | AD 100
Lifting machines first
used for building |

SKYSCRAPERS

ABOVE Chicago's Home Insurance Building designed by Jenney.

When were skyscrapers invented?

In 1885, a 10-storey-high office building in Chicago became the first of many skyscrapers. The American architect William le Baron Jenney first got the idea on a trip to Southeast Asia. Here, he saw houses made of reed matting strung on a framework of tree-trunks. Jenney built the first high-rise building with a metal frame to support the floors and walls. This type of tall building quickly became known as a skyscraper.

LEFT The famous Empire State Building in New York, USA, was the world's tallest building when it was first built in 1931.

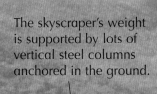

The skyscraper's weight is supported by lots of vertical steel columns anchored in the ground.

How are skyscrapers built?

In a brick or stone building, the walls of the ground floor have to hold up the weight of the rest of the structure. This means that even very thick walls can only support a building up to five storeys high. Skyscrapers have an incredibly strong steel framework, rather like a skeleton, to carry the weight of the building. Lightweight walls slot into or hang from this framework.

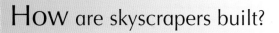

Each floor is formed from steel girders that run horizontally between the columns.

DID YOU KNOW?
Most modern skyscrapers are built with self-cleaning glass, so there is no need for window cleaners. The glass has a special coating that stops dirt from sticking to it.

What is the world's tallest building?

The Taipei 101 in Taiwan is the world's tallest building. Completed in 2004, this skyscraper is over half a kilometre high and boasts a record 101 floors. The skyscraper is specially strengthened to withstand earthquakes, typhoons and high winds.

RIGHT The Taipei 101 has the world's fastest lifts, which travel upwards at a speed of 1,008 metres a minute. They whisk passengers to the top of the building in just 30 seconds!

The outer layer of glass and concrete is often called the curtain wall because of the way it hangs from the framework.

Who invented electric lifts?

The first powered elevator, or lift, was built in 1857 by the American Elisha Graves Otis for a New York department store. By 1903, the Otis company had perfected an electric lift that made high-rise buildings a practical possibility. When passengers got in the lift, a pulley system moved it up and down a shaft inside the building. Steel cables from the lift looped round a wheel, driven by an electric motor.

motorized wheel

steel cables

lift

counterweight

LEFT The lift cables are joined to a heavy counterweight, which balances the load.

67

BUILDING KEY DATES

| 4000 BC First canals in use | 3500 BC First oven-baked clay bricks | 2000 BC Clapper bridges used to cross rivers | 700 BC First aqueduct built to carry water | AD 100 Lifting machines first used for building |

BRIDGES

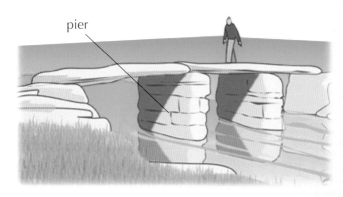

pier

ABOVE A stone clapper bridge

When were the first bridges built?

The earliest water crossings were logs laid over streams, but these simple beam bridges could not span wide rivers. People first built stone clapper bridges around 2000 BC. Slabs of stone were piled up in a river to make piers. The piers supported larger, flat stones that spanned the gaps and formed a pathway over the water.

Who invented arched bridges?

The Romans first used stone arches in their buildings and monuments. They soon realized that arches make strong structures and could be used to support bridges, too. Today's arched bridges are often made of steel or concrete and can span much wider gaps.

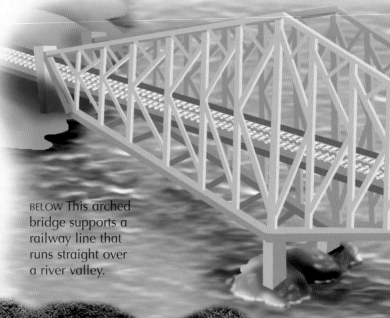

BELOW This arched bridge supports a railway line that runs straight over a river valley.

What is a suspension bridge?

Thousands of years ago, people in South America and Asia built simple rope bridges to help them cross rivers or canyons. Modern suspension bridges work in a similar way. The deck, or roadway, of a suspension bridge hangs from two main steel cables attached to tall support towers on both sides of the river. Wire hanger cables link the main cables to the deck.

BELOW A suspension bridge, like the Brooklyn Bridge in New York, USA, is the best kind of bridge for spanning a wide crossing.

tower   main cable

People, trains, and traffic move across the deck.

BELOW The world's longest cantilever bridge is the Quebec Railway Bridge in Canada.

Built in 1917, the steel bridge spans 549 metres.

How are cantilever bridges built?

Cantilever bridges were invented to span wider rivers than beam and arched bridges. They have a rigid metal framework that is divided into sections made up of strong, straight steel tubes arranged in triangular shapes. Each section is supported in the middle by a pier in the river, so that the weight of the bridge is balanced out.

DID YOU KNOW?
The Akashi Kaikyo Bridge in Japan is the world's longest suspension bridge. It has a main span of 1,990 metres.

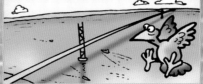

Each half of the bridge balances on a supporting pier.

69

ENERGY KEY DATES

600 BC	30 BC	AD 1712	1800	1831
Windmill invented to grind flour	Water wheels used to power water mills	First steam engine invented	Battery first used to produce electricity	Electrical generator invented

STEAM POWER

When was the steam engine invented?

In 1712, a steam-powered piston engine was developed for the first time by the Englishman Thomas Newcomen. His engine burnt coal to make steam. The steam powered pumps, which removed floodwater from mines.

How did steam engines work?

In 1769, the Scottish engineer James Watt improved Newcomen's steam engine. In Watt's engine, the steam was forced into a cylinder pushing the piston up. The steam was then condensed by a jet of cold water. This created a vacuum, which let the piston fall back down the cylinder. The up-and-down movement of the piston could power pumps or drive a rocking beam, which turned the wheels of all kinds of factory machines.

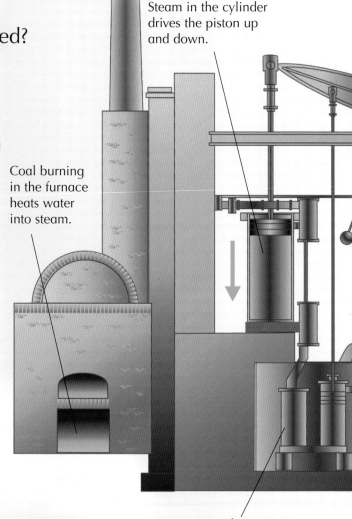

BELOW Watt's steam engine

Steam in the cylinder drives the piston up and down.

Coal burning in the furnace heats water into steam.

condenser

LEFT Steam engines were later modified to power railway locomotives and steamships.

75029

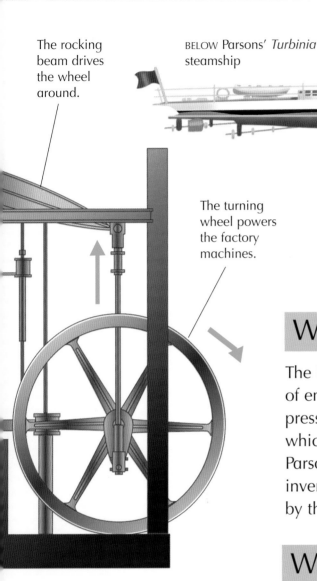

The rocking beam drives the wheel around.

The turning wheel powers the factory machines.

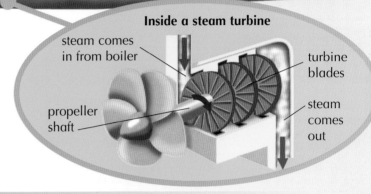

BELOW Parsons' *Turbinia* steamship

Inside a steam turbine

steam comes in from boiler

turbine blades

propeller shaft

steam comes out

Who invented the steam turbine?

The English engineer Charles Parsons built a new kind of engine called the steam turbine in 1884. High-pressure steam rotated a series of turbine blades, which generated the power to drive machines. In 1897, Parsons launched his steamship, the *Turbinia,* to test his invention. The ship raced through the water powered by three turbine engines turning nine propellers.

What fuels today's steam-powered cars?

In 2004, British engineers produced *Inspiration*, a fast, futuristic car propelled by a jet of steam. Steam-driven engines can use any fuel, including solar energy. This means they make fewer polluting exhaust fumes. In the future, designers hope that steam-powered cars might be an environmentally friendly alternative to vehicles with petrol engines.

RIGHT *Inspiration* has a steam engine that runs on propane gas.

DID YOU KNOW?
In 1906, a steam-powered car, called the *Stanley Rocket*, set the world land-speed record at 205 kilometres (128 miles) per hour. The record still stands for steam-powered cars today.

71

ENERGY KEY DATES

| 600 BC
Windmill invented
to grind flour | 30 BC
Water wheels used
to power water mills | AD 1712
First steam engine
invented | 1800
Battery first used to
produce electricity | 1831
Electrical generator
invented |

ELECTRICITY

Who invented the battery?

In 1780, the Italian scientist Alessandro Volta realized that a chemical reaction between a dead frog, a metal knife and a metal table created an electric charge that made the dead frog jolt! Later, in 1800, Volta made the first battery from a pile of zinc and copper discs separated by cloth soaked in salt water. When connected, a chemical reaction between the metals and the salt water produced an electric current.

RIGHT Volta's pile battery

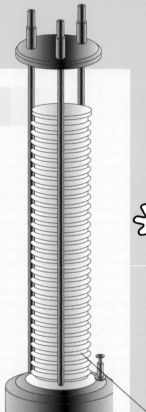

pairs of zinc and copper discs

> **DID YOU KNOW?**
> Batteries may soon be replaced by non-polluting fuel cells. These convert the gases hydrogen and oxygen into water to produce electricity.

BELOW Faraday also built the first electromagnetic generator, using a fixed magnet, in 1832.

A copper disc rotates between the poles of a magnet.

A small electric current flows through the wire.

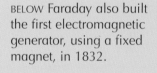

magnet

What is an electrical generator?

In 1831, the English scientist Michael Faraday demonstrated the first simple electrical generator. By moving a magnet through a loop of copper wire, the magnetism generated an electric current, which flowed through the wire. It was another 50 years before the first large generator providing mains electric power was built. This used a spinning magnet inside a giant coil of metal wire to create an electric current.

A voltmeter measures the strength of the electric current.

When was the electric light invented?

It was only when the light bulb was invented, in 1879, that it became possible to light buildings with electricity. A light bulb is a glass globe with a wire inside, called a filament. The filament glows when electricity passes through it and produces light. Electric lamps first became reliable when the American inventor Thomas Edison discovered the carbon filament. This produced light for a long period of time before burning out.

filament

How do we get our electricity?

A coal-fired powered station burns coal in a furnace to boil water into steam. The high-pressure steam drives turbines linked to large electrical generators. These convert the spinning movement of the turbines into electrical energy, which is carried along power lines to homes, factories and businesses.

RIGHT Electricity flows along cables either buried in the ground or carried by tall towers called pylons.

cooling towers

turbine and generator house

coal store

ENERGY KEY DATES

600 BC	30 BC	AD 1712	1800	1831
Windmill invented to grind flour	Water wheels used to power water mills	First steam engine invented	Battery first used to produce electricity	Electrical generator invented

NUCLEAR POWER

Who first split the atom?

In 1938, the German scientists Otto Hahn and Fritz Strassmann first discovered they could split the atom of a rare metal called uranium-235. Atoms are tiny particles of matter that can be seen only under a powerful microscope. When the uranium atoms started to split, or fission, they released huge amounts of heat energy. As the atom fragments hit other atoms, they also split and created more heat in a chain reaction – producing nuclear energy for the first time.

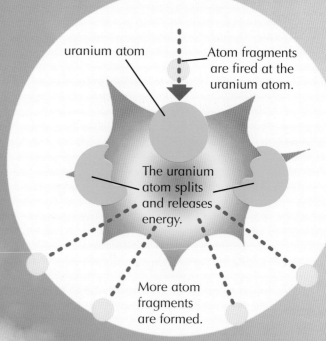

uranium atom

Atom fragments are fired at the uranium atom.

The uranium atom splits and releases energy.

More atom fragments are formed.

ABOVE Atoms can be split to create nuclear energy.

BELOW A modern-day nuclear power station.

steam cooling tower

nuclear reactor

Where was nuclear power first made?

In 1951, electricity was generated using the heat energy from a nuclear fission reactor for the very first time. It was produced by a group of American scientists working at a lonely nuclear experiment station in the deserts of Idaho. The first nuclear power station to supply mains electricity was opened in the former Soviet Union in 1954.

How do nuclear fuel rods work?

Nuclear power stations run on uranium fuel. Pellets of uranium are stacked inside metal fuel rods. The fuel rods are gathered together in bundles and placed in a reactor full of water, surrounded by control rods. When the control rods are raised out of the reactor, the uranium atoms start to split, or fission, and the water temperature begins to rise. The boiling water is used to make steam, which drives turbines linked to electrical generators.

Control rods are raised or lowered to control the nuclear reaction.

The fuel rods are grouped into bundles and placed underwater in the reactor.

uranium pellets inside a fuel rod

DID YOU KNOW?
Nuclear-powered naval submarines can cruise non-stop for 25 years without needing to refuel.

What makes nuclear power safe?

Uranium gives off harmful radiation as well as heat during nuclear fission. So nuclear power reactors are built out of several layers of very thick metal and concrete. This prevents radioactive material from escaping into the environment. Used nuclear fuel rods are also highly radioactive. They are cooled down in water for many years, before being loaded into special containers and carefully transported by road or rail to a disposal site. Here, the radioactive waste is buried in tunnels deep underground, well away from people.

dry, stable rock

shaft

The fuel rods are buried in tunnels.

Nuclear waste remains radioactive underground for about 1,000 years.

LEFT Isolated disposal sites were invented as a means of dealing with high-level radioactive waste.

ENERGY KEY DATES

600 BC	**30** BC	**AD 1712**	**1800**	**1831**
Windmill invented to grind flour	Water wheels used to power water mills	First steam engine invented	Battery first used to produce electricity	Electrical generator invented

NATURAL ENERGY SOURCES

A small electrical generator is positioned behind the blades.

turbine blades

When were wind turbines invented?

Wind turbines were first used in the 1940s to turn the natural energy of the wind into electricity. They powered remote farms in the USA. Today's wind turbines have two or three propeller-like blades, which are mounted on tall towers up to 30 metres high. As the wind blows, the turbine blades rotate and drive a small generator that produces electricity. Since the early 1980s, groups of wind turbines, called wind farms, have been built both on land and out at sea.

How is natural waste used as fuel?

Waste materials from plants, such as wood chips, sawdust from sawmills, or straw from farms, are called biomass fuels. Biogas can also be made from animal waste, such as manure. These fuels can be burned to heat water and make steam for power stations.

BELOW A digester produces biogas from animal manure. The manure is stored in a tank for a few weeks, where it rots and gives off gas.

Biogas is collected from the top of the digester.

Inside a wind turbine

driveshaft

gears

electricity generator

A drive turns the blades to face into the wind.

turbine blade

Left-over manure is piped out of the tank.

Where was the first tidal power station?

The movement of the sea carries energy in the form of tides, currents and waves. A tidal power station uses this natural energy to produce electricity. The world's first and largest-ever tidal power station was opened in 1966 on the River Rance in France. A huge dam, called a barrage, was built across the river estuary where it meets the sea. As the tides come in and go out, the water flows through tunnels in the barrage, turning turbines that drive electricity generators.

LEFT The River Rance tidal barrage in France

DID YOU KNOW?
Scientists have invented a way of turning pig manure into biomass diesel to power cars. One pig could produce around 80 litres of diesel in a lifetime.

What is geothermal energy?

The temperatures in the centre of the Earth are hot enough to melt rock. In some places, this molten rock is not far below ground and generates natural heat, called geothermal energy. Wells are drilled into the ground and cold water is pumped down to the hot rocks. The water heats up and turns into steam. This is piped back above ground and used to turn turbines that drive electricity generators.

geothermal power station

Steam is piped back to the power station.

Cold water is pumped down to the hot rocks.

hot, molten rock

SPACE

From our first glimpses of space through early telescopes to space travel today, inventions have been the only way that we could find out more about the Universe beyond our planet. Discover where the *Hubble* Space Telescope is, how rockets fly and why satellites can stay in orbit around the Earth. Learn about astronauts who space walk in the empty weightlessness of outer space around their space shuttles, or live in space stations for months at a time. Read about the space probes travelling into deep space to investigate parts of the Universe never before explored.

SPACE KEY DATES

AD 1608	1926	1957	1961	1962
First successful refracting telescope	Liquid-fuel rocket invented	Rocket took the first satellite into space	First successful space capsule	First space probe to reach another planet

TELESCOPES

LEFT Galileo Galilei at his telescope

Who first invented the telescope?

The Dutch spectacle maker Hans Lippershey made the first successful refracting telescope in 1608. He realized that by looking through two lenses, placed at each end of a tube, far-away objects appeared larger. By 1609, the Italian scientist Galileo Galilei was using a similar telescope to study the night sky. He used it to map the surface of the Moon and discover the planet Jupiter's four moons.

How does a reflecting telescope work?

A reflecting telescope uses mirrors to help astronomers see a brighter and clearer view of distant stars and planets. The English scientist Isaac Newton designed and built the first reflecting telescope in 1668. The telescope collects light rays from an object on a curved mirror at one end. The mirror reflects, or bounces, the rays onto a flat, angled mirror to form an image. A lens then magnifies this image in the viewing eyepiece.

RIGHT Newton's reflecting telescope

DID YOU KNOW?
Some of the largest reflecting telescopes in the world are on the island of Hawaii, USA. The twin 10 metre Keck telescopes sit over 4,000 metres high on top of Mauna Kea, an extinct volcano.

lens

eyepiece

curved mirror

light rays

Inside a reflecting telescope

flat, angled mirror

What is a radio telescope?

Astronomers use a radio telescope linked to computers to detect radio waves and create pictures of distant space objects. As well as radio waves, space objects such as black holes and galaxies also give out gamma rays, infra-red, ultraviolet and X-rays, which people cannot see. These can be detected by special sorts of telescope. The atmosphere blocks out most of these waves, so they are usually observed from artificial satellites, above the atmosphere.

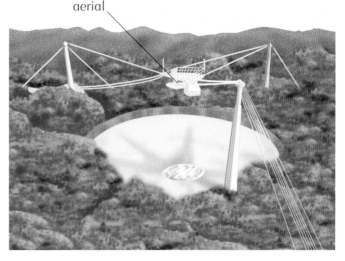

aerial

ABOVE The Arecibo radio telescope in Puerto Rico has a single, giant dish. This collects and directs radio waves from space onto a receiving aerial.

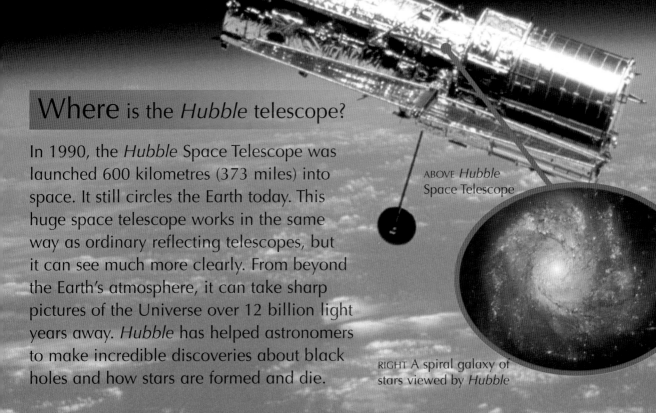

ABOVE *Hubble* Space Telescope

Where is the *Hubble* telescope?

In 1990, the *Hubble* Space Telescope was launched 600 kilometres (373 miles) into space. It still circles the Earth today. This huge space telescope works in the same way as ordinary reflecting telescopes, but it can see much more clearly. From beyond the Earth's atmosphere, it can take sharp pictures of the Universe over 12 billion light years away. *Hubble* has helped astronomers to make incredible discoveries about black holes and how stars are formed and die.

RIGHT A spiral galaxy of stars viewed by *Hubble*

81

SPACE KEY DATES

| AD 1608
First successful
refracting telescope | 1926
Liquid-fuel rocket
invented | 1957
Rocket took the first
satellite into space | 1961
First successful
space capsule | 1962
First space probe to
reach another planet |

ROCKETS

LEFT Rockets transport astronauts, satellites or research equipment into space.

The launchpad scaffolding supports the rocket until lift-off.

When were rockets first built?

The first gunpowder rockets were made by the Chinese around 1,000 years ago and used as fireworks or weapons. In 1926, the American scientist Robert Goddard built the first controllable rocket that ran on liquid fuel – a mixture of petrol and oxygen.

What is a space rocket?

A space rocket is a high-speed, cylinder-shaped engine powerful enough to overcome the pull of Earth's gravity and carry objects into space. Space rockets need to carry enormous tanks of fuel. The burning fuel produces a jet of hot waste gases that lifts the rocket off the ground. The first rocket powerful enough to reach space was a weapon invented by the German engineer Wernher von Braun in 1942.

BELOW Von Braun's unmanned *V-2* rocket missile was used to bomb Britain during World War II.

How do rockets fly?

When you blow up a balloon, then let it go without tying the end, the balloon is thrust forwards by the escaping jet of air. This is how a rocket flies into space. A rocket burns fuel with liquid oxygen to make a powerful jet of very hot exhaust gases. This shoots out of the bottom of the rocket, lifting it into the air at high speed.

The pointed nose cone cuts through the air.

The payload is what the rocket is designed to carry – the cargo and astronauts.

rocket guidance system

liquid fuel tank

liquid oxygen tank

pumps

The combustion engine is where the fuel burns.

exhaust nozzles

The tail fins keep the rocket stable during flight.

DID YOU KNOW?
Saturn V, which carried the USA's *Apollo* spacecraft to the Moon, was one of the biggest rockets ever to be invented. It was as tall as a 30-storey skyscraper and as powerful as 150 jumbo jets.

BELOW Space rockets are made up of a number of different stages, which fall away once the fuel is used up.

Stage three carries the payload into orbit. Once the satellite or spacecraft is launched, the rocket's work is done.

Stage two engines then take over. They burn liquid fuel, which thrusts the rocket upwards.

Stage one contains solid fuel rocket boosters which burn to give lift-off.

Who sent the first rocket into orbit?

The first rocket to put an object into orbit was launched by the Soviet Union in 1957. It carried the first space satellite called *Sputnik 1*. During the 1960s, Soviet and American scientists developed 'multi-stage' rockets. These carried manned spacecraft into orbit round the Earth. They were made up of several different sections. Each had its own engine and a fuel and oxygen supply, which enabled the rockets to travel further into space.

SPACE KEY DATES

AD **1608**	**1926**	**1957**	**1961**	**1962**
First successful refracting telescope	Liquid-fuel rocket invented	Rocket took the first satellite into space	First successful space capsule	First space probe to reach another planet

SATELLITES

DID YOU KNOW?

Old satellites and discarded rocket parts are left to float around in space. Scientists estimate that there are now around 70,000 pieces of 'space junk' orbiting the Earth.

When was the first satellite invented?

A satellite is anything that orbits, or circles, a larger object in space, such as the Moon orbiting the Earth. But the first artificial satellite, called *Sputnik I,* was invented by Soviet scientists in 1957. Once in orbit, this simple satellite measured the temperature of the Earth's atmosphere. It sent back the information using radio signals.

ABOVE RIGHT
Sputnik I satellite

BELOW The speed of the moving satellite balances the downward pull of gravity to keep it in orbit.

Why do satellites stay in orbit?

Most satellites move in almost circular orbits a few hundred kilometres above the Earth. Gravity is almost as strong there as it is at the surface, and pulls the satellite downwards. The satellite is constantly falling towards the centre of the Earth. But because of its sideways motion, and the curvature of the Earth, the satellite circles the planet at the same height. Even satellites thousands of kilometres above the Earth are held in orbit by Earth's gravity.

How do satellites work?

Most satellites are powered by solar panels, which convert sunlight into electricity. Small rocket thrusters move and turn the satellites. Sensors check they are facing in the right direction. All satellites have communication aerials, radio receivers and transmitters to receive signals and send messages to ground stations back on Earth. Satellites also carry specific instruments depending on the job they are intended to do.

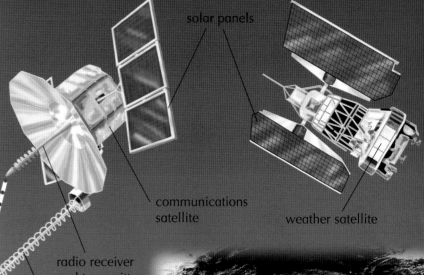

solar panels

communications satellite

weather satellite

radio receiver and transmitter

communication aerial

RIGHT A weather satellite has onboard cameras to take photographs of cloud formations, such as this hurricane. These are sent to weather-forecasting stations back on Earth.

BELOW Ground stations send and receive signals from large dishes pointed at satellites in space.

What are satellites used for?

There are several different kinds of satellites in space, each doing different jobs. As well as weather satellites, there are communication satellites, which broadcast television and telephone signals all over the world. Some satellites send back photographs, which are used to make maps. Others provide information about the Earth and the Universe to help with scientific investigations. Navigation satellites help people to find their way and pinpoint exact locations on Earth.

SPACE KEY DATES

| AD 1608 | 1926 | 1957 | 1961 | 1962 |
| First successful refracting telescope | Liquid-fuel rocket invented | Rocket took the first satellite into space | First successful space capsule | First space probe to reach another planet |

SPACECRAFT

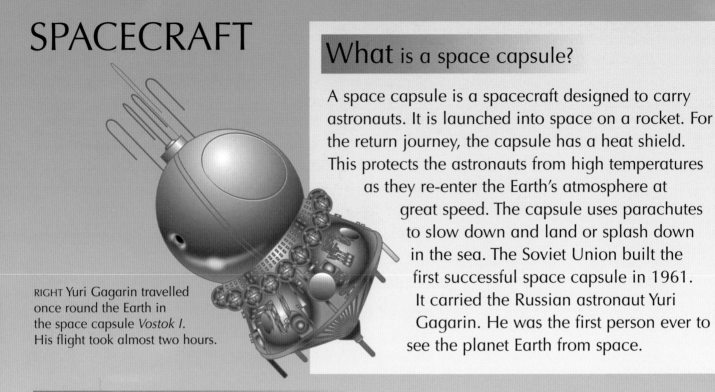

RIGHT Yuri Gagarin travelled once round the Earth in the space capsule *Vostok I*. His flight took almost two hours.

What is a space capsule?

A space capsule is a spacecraft designed to carry astronauts. It is launched into space on a rocket. For the return journey, the capsule has a heat shield. This protects the astronauts from high temperatures as they re-enter the Earth's atmosphere at great speed. The capsule uses parachutes to slow down and land or splash down in the sea. The Soviet Union built the first successful space capsule in 1961. It carried the Russian astronaut Yuri Gagarin. He was the first person ever to see the planet Earth from space.

Which spacecraft first landed on the Moon?

In 1969, American astronauts were carried to the Moon in the *Apollo 11* spacecraft. Neil Armstrong and Edwin 'Buzz' Aldrin left the spacecraft orbiting the Moon and travelled down to land on the Moon's surface in a small lunar module.

BELOW Armstrong and Aldrin were the first men ever to walk on the Moon.

lunar module

DID YOU KNOW?
Scientists invented special protective suits for the Space Shuttle astronauts to use when 'space walking'. They wear them outside the spacecraft when repairing satellites or servicing the *Hubble* space telescope.

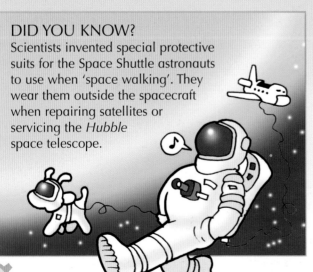

The Shuttle orbiter carries the crew and cargo into space and brings them back to Earth. It is used for several space missions.

Why was the Space Shuttle invented?

Space Shuttles were designed as the first reusable spacecraft. A space capsule transported by rocket can be used only on one journey. But Space Shuttles transport astronauts and science equipment into space to carry out investigations or launch satellites, then they fly back to Earth to be used again. The USA launched the first Space Shuttle, *Columbia*, in 1981.

The external fuel tank burns up after use and cannot be reused.

BELOW The Space Shuttle is launched into space like a rocket. It acts like a spacecraft in space, then glides back to Earth like an aeroplane.

Two solid-fuel rocket boosters are used for lift-off and then recycled for use in other missions.

How is the Space Shuttle reused?

New fuel tanks are added to a Space Shuttle on each new mission. At lift-off, two solid-fuel rocket boosters launch the Shuttle orbiter. Once this fuel is used up, the rocket boosters fall away and parachute into the ocean. These are collected and used again. The liquid fuel tank comes away later, but burns up in Earth's atmosphere. The Shuttle carries the astronauts and equipment into orbit where it circles the Earth. On its return journey, the Shuttle lands like a giant aeroplane on a runway.

SPACE KEY DATES

AD **1608** First successful refracting telescope	**1926** Liquid-fuel rocket invented	**1957** Rocket took the first satellite into space	**1961** First successful space capsule	**1962** First space probe to reach another planet

SPACE STATIONS

DID YOU KNOW?
A space station is a weightless environment. This means that astronauts have to eat their meals and drink from special sealed bags. Otherwise their food would start to float around in the air!

Who launched the first space station?

In 1971, the Soviet Union launched the first-ever space station, *Salyut 1*. This research laboratory was designed to remain in space, orbiting the Earth. Three astronauts travelled up to the station in the spacecraft *Soyuz II*. The crew set the first space duration record by staying onboard for 22 days. After five months in space, the station fell back to Earth and burned up as it re-entered the Earth's atmosphere.

BELOW *Soyuz II* docking with *Salyut 1*

How many space stations have there been?

The Russians put six successful *Salyut* stations into orbit between 1971 and 1982. *Skylab* was launched by the USA in 1973. In 1986, the Russians launched a larger space station called *Mir*. All these space stations have since either fallen back to Earth or been removed from orbit at the end of their use.

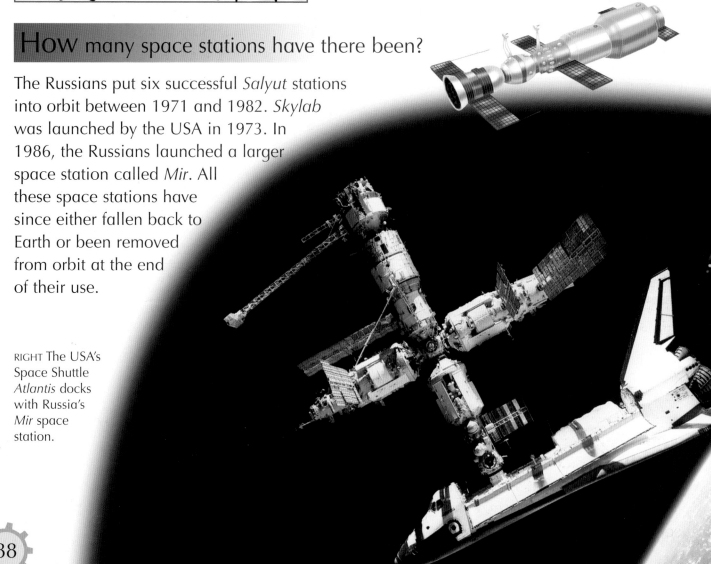

RIGHT The USA's Space Shuttle *Atlantis* docks with Russia's *Mir* space station.

solar panels

research laboratory

ABOVE Planned for completion in 2010, the ISS will be the biggest space station ever built.

RIGHT Scientists from different countries carry out experiments in the research laboratories of the International Space Station.

What is the ISS?

In 1998, several countries worked together to design the International Space Station, or ISS. The ISS is so big, it has to be built in sections and assembled out in space by astronauts. The station has huge, wing-shaped solar panels, which collect energy from the Sun to power all the onboard machines. There is a generator for making oxygen, so that the astronauts can breathe and there are systems to clean and purify the water. Spacecraft delivering new crew members, supplies and equipment link up with the station at docking ports.

BELOW An astronaut 'space walking'.

Why were space stations invented?

Astronauts carry out scientific research in laboratories onboard space stations. From space, it is easier to study the Universe and observe the Earth's weather systems. Some scientists investigate how the human body is affected by living in a weightless environment, where astronauts and objects float around inside the space station. Scientists also test materials that might one day be used to build spacecraft to carry people to other planets, like Mars.

SPACE KEY DATES

| AD **1608** First successful refracting telescope | **1926** Liquid-fuel rocket invented | **1957** Rocket took the first satellite into space | **1961** First successful space capsule | **1962** First space probe to reach another planet |

SPACE PROBES

Who built the first space probe?

The Russian *Lunik I* was the first space probe to be launched in 1959, but it failed to reach its target, the Moon. Space probes are unmanned spacecraft that are launched deep into space. They either fly past, orbit or land on planets and collect information about them. In 1962, the USA's *Mariner 2* probe flew by Venus, making it the first spacecraft to successfully encounter another planet.

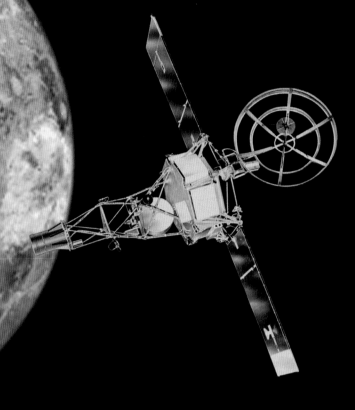

RIGHT The *Mariner 2* space probe investigated the planet Venus.

Venus

Why do we need space probes?

Space probes are loaded with high-tech equipment and scientific instruments to gather data on distant planets. Once the spacecraft reach their target planet, the equipment switches on. It starts to take accurate pictures, record measurements and collect mapping information, which is transmitted back to scientists on Earth. Apart from Pluto – the farthest planet from the Sun – all of the planets in our solar system have now been explored.

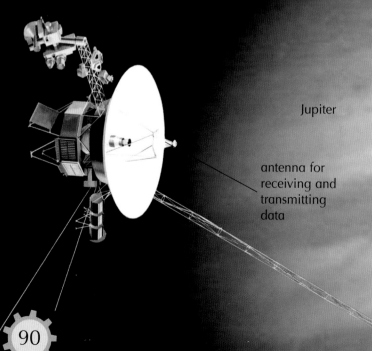

Jupiter

antenna for receiving and transmitting data

LEFT The *Voyager 2* is the only space probe to have flown past four different planets – Jupiter, Saturn, Uranus and Neptune.

969
irst spacecraft to
and on the Moon

1971
Launch of the
first space station

1981
First flight of the
Space Shuttle

1983
First space probe to
leave the solar system

1990
Launch of the first
space telescope

What is the *Cassini-Huygens* probe?

The *Cassini-Huygens* space probe was
launched in 1997 to investigate the planet
Saturn. The spacecraft reached Saturn's orbit
in 2004. From here, *Cassini* began a four-
year study of the planet, its atmosphere,
its rings and many moons. The
smaller probe, *Huygens*, was
later released by the main
spacecraft. It successfully
landed on Titan,
Saturn's largest
moon.

BELOW The *Cassini-Huygens* space
probe is one of the largest ever built.
It's about as big as a 30-seater bus.

Saturn

Neptune

How far can space probes travel?

As there are no astronauts on board,
scientists can risk sending probes out into
deep space to investigate unknown parts of
the Universe. The first space probe to leave
our solar system was *Pioneer 10* in 1983.
Space probes such as this travel for many
years and for millions of kilometres into
outer space. No one really knows what they
may discover there in the future.

DID YOU KNOW?

In January 2006, *Stardust* became
the first space probe to collect and
send back dust samples
from a comet in outer
space. Scientists
believe the tiny
fragments were formed
about 4.5 billion
years ago!

Uranus

91

INDEX

A

aeroplanes 16, 60-61
Akashi Kaikyo
    Bridge 69
aluminium 23
arched bridges 68
Archimedean screw 15
Archimedes 6, 15
Arkwright, Richard 21
assembly lines 24-25
atoms 74

B

Babbage, Charles 44
Baekeland, Leo 22
Baird, John Logie 50
Bakelite 22
bar codes 37
batteries 72
battery-powered
    cars 55
Baylis, Trevor 42
Bell, Alexander
    Graham 40
Benz, Karl 54
Bezos, Jeff 37

bicycles 62-63
biomass fuels 76, 77
books 38
Booth, Cecil 34
Braun, Wernher
    von 82
bridges 68-69
Brunel, Marc Isambard
    24

C

camera film 46
camera obscura 46
cameras 46-47
cantilever bridges 69
cars 24, 54-55, 71
cash registers 36
Cassini-Huygens space
    probe 91
catapults 6
caterpillar tracks 11
cathode ray tubes 50
celluloid 22
central heating 28
cheese-making 13
cinema 48-49

clockwork radios 42
Colvin, L.O. 12
combine harvesters 11
computer-animated
    movies 48
computers 44-45
cookers 32
Cooper, Martin 41
cotton gins 20
Crompton, Bell 29
crop watering 14-15
cropdusters 16
cruise liners 59

D

Daimler, Gottlieb 63
department stores 36
desk-top publishing 39
detergents 22, 31
digital cameras 47
digital radios 43
digital television 51
dishwashers 31
Dowsing, Herbert 29
Drebbel, Cornelius 64
Dunlop, John 62

E

Eastman, George 46

Eckert, John 44

Edison, Thomas 73

Einstein, Albert 7

electric cookers 32

electric irons 34

electric telegraph 40

electricity 72-73, 74

Empire State
  Building 66

F

factories 21, 24-25

Faraday, Michael 72

farm chemicals 16-17

fertilizers 16, 17

Fessenden, Reginald 42

fire 6

Fisher, Alva J. 30

flat panel TVs 51

flying shuttles 20

food processors 35

Ford, Henry 54

fridge-freezers 33

Froehlich, John 10

fuel cells 72

fungicides 16

G

Galileo Galilei 80

gas cookers 32

gas fires 28

generators 72, 73, 75,
  77

genetically modified
  (GM) foods 18-19

geothermal energy 77

Goddard, Robert 82

Gutenberg, Johann 38

H

Hadaway, William 32

Hahn, Otto 74

hairdryers 35

Hargreaves, James 20

Heinkel, Ernst 60

Henry, Joseph 40

herbicides 16

Holland, John P. 64

Hubble telescope 81

I

IMAX 3D cinemas 49

insecticides 16, 17

internal combustion
  engines 54

International Space
  Station (ISS) 89

Internet shopping 37

J

Jenney, William le Baron
  66

jet engines 60

Jobs, Steve 44

jump jets 61

K

Kamem, Dean 7

Kay, John 20

L

laptops 45

laser printers 39

Leonardo da Vinci 7

Leoni, Sigismund 28

levers 6, 63

lifts (elevators) 67
light bulbs 73
Lippershey, Hans 80
looms 20, 21
Lumière, Auguste and
    Louis 48

M

Maglev trains 57
Marconi, Guglielmo 42
mass customization 25
mass production 24-25
matches 6
Mauchly, John 44
Maybach, Wilhelm 63
microchips 7, 45
microwave ovens 32
milking machines 12, 13
mobile phones 41
monorail trains 56
Morse, Samuel 40
Morse code 40, 42
motorbikes 63
mouse traps 6
Müller, Paul 16

N

natural energy 76-77

navigation satellites 85
Newcomen, Thomas 70
Niépce, Joseph 46
nuclear fuel rods 75
nuclear power 7, 64,
    74-75
nutcrackers 6

O

Olds, Ransom E. 24
organic farming 17
Otis, Elisha Graves 67

P

paddle steamers 58
Parsons, Charles 58, 71
passenger ferries 59
Pasteur, Louis 13
pasteurization 13
patents 7
penny farthings 62
personal computers
    (PCs) 44
pesticides 16, 17
pivot and drip irrigation
    15
plastic 22, 23
Plunkett, Roy 6

pneumatic tyres 11, 62
power stations 73, 74,
    75, 77
printing presses 38, 39

R

racing cars 55
radiators 29
radio telescopes 81
radios 42-43
refrigerators 33
Ritty, James 36
robots 13, 25
rockets 82-83

S

sailing ships 58
satellite TV 51
satellites 51, 83, 84-85
scissors 6
Seely, Henry W. 34
Segway Human
    Transporter 7
shaduf 14
Sharp, James 32
ships 58-59, 71
Sholes, Christopher 38
shopping 36-37

Silly Putty 6
skyscrapers 66-67
Slinky Toy 6
SLR cameras 47
soap 23, 31
solar panels 85, 89
space capsules 86
space probes 90-91
Space Shuttles 87
space stations 88-89
spacecraft 83, 86-87
spacesuits 86
Spencer, Percy 32
spinning jenny 20
spinning wheels 20
Starley, John 62
steam engines 56, 70
steam-powered cars 71
steamships 71
Stephenson, George
    56
Strassmann, Fritz 74
submarines 7, 64-65,
    75
submersibles 64
supermarkets 36
supersonic planes 61
supertankers 59
suspension bridges
    69

T
Taipei 101 skyscraper
    67
Teflon 6
telephones 40-41
telescopes 80-81
television 50-51
TGV trains 57
tidal power stations 77
toasters 34
torpedoes 65
traction engines 10
tractors 10-11
trademarks 7
trains 56-57
transistor radios 43
turbines 71, 73, 75, 76
tweezers 6
typewriters 38

U
underground railways 57

V
vacuum cleaners 6, 34
Vail, Alfred 40
videophones 40
Volta, Alessandro 72

W
washing machines 30
Watt, James 70
weather satellites 85
Whitehead, Robert 65
Whitney, Eli 20
Whittle, Frank 60
wind farms 76
Wozniak, Steve 44
Wright, Wilbur and
    Orville 60
wringers 31

Z
Zworykin, Vladimir 50

ACKNOWLEDGEMENTS

Artwork supplied through the SGA Illustration Agency by Geoff Ball and James Alexander

Photo credits:
b = bottom, t = top, r = right, l = left, m = middle

Front cover: Charles O'Rear/Corbis, tl (inset) Stockdisc/Corbis, tm (inset) Digital Vision/Getty Images, tr (inset) Liz Barry/
Eye Ubiquitous/Corbis
Back cover: Getty Images
Front flap: NASA
Back flap: David Frazier/Corbis

Running head band Photodisc/Getty Images, 1 Stockdisc Photos/Getty Images, 2 Comstock, 3l Photodisc/Getty Images,
3m Rick Fredman/Corbis, 3r Paul Saunders/Corbis, 4 NASA, 6 Comstock/Jupiter Images, 6bl Bettman /Corbis, 7tl
Bettman/Corbis, 7tr Bettman/Corbis, 7br Rick Fredman/Corbis, 8 Brand X Pictures/Jupiter Images, 9l Brand X Pictures/
Jupiter Images, 9m David Frazier/Corbis, 9r David Frazier/Corbis, 10 Corbis, 11 David Frazier/Corbis, 12 David Frazier/
Corbis, 14 Reed Kaestner/Corbis, 15 David Frazier/Corbis, 16/17 Warren Jacobi/Corbis, 18l Richard Gross/Corbis, 18r
David Frazier/Corbis, 19 David Frazier/Corbis, 21l Flat Earth, 21r Brand X Pictures/Jupiter Images, 22 Digital Vision/
Getty Images, 23t Brand X Pictures/Jupiter Images, 23b Digital Vision/Getty Images, 25m Photodisc/Getty Images, 25b
Banana Stock/Jupiter Images, 26 Digital Vision/Getty Images, 27lm Digital Vision/Getty Images, 27r Photodisc/Getty
Images, 28 Digital Vision/Getty Images, 29 Comstock/Jupiter Images, 30 Randy Faris/Corbis, 31l Digital Vision/Getty
Images, 31r Image Source, 32 Lawrence Manning/Corbis, 33 Randy Faris/Corbis, 34 Comstock/Jupiter Images, 35t
Lawrence Manning/Corbis, 35b Photodisc/Getty Images, 36 Brand X Pictures/Jupiter Images, 37 Ben Blankenburg/
Corbis, 38 Comstock/Jupiter Images, 39t Getty Images, 39b StockDisc/Corbis, 40 Comstock/Jupiter Images, 41l (inset)
StockDisc/Corbis, 41 Banana Stock/Jupiter Images, 42 Comstock/Corbis, 43t Classic PIO, 43r David Frazier/Corbis, 45tr
Reed Kaestner/Corbis. 45l (inset) Photodisc/Getty Images, 45r (inset) StockDisc/Corbis, 46 Comstock/Jupiter Images, 46t
Comstock/Jupiter Images, 47t Banana Stock/Jupiter Images, 47b Comstock/Jupiter Images, 48/49 ImageState, 49t
Comstock/Jupiter Images, 50 Comstock/Jupiter Images, 51t Bloomimage/Corbis, 51b Banana Stock/Jupiter Images, 52
Brand X Pictures/Jupiter Images, 53l Brand X Pictures/Jupiter Images, 53m Image Ideas/Index Stock Imagery, Inc., 53r
Photodisc/Getty Images, 54 Brand X Pictures/Jupiter Images, 55t Brand X Pictures/Jupiter Images, 55m Leo Dennis
Productions/Brand /Corbis, 56 Digital Vision/Getty Images, 57 Paul Saunders/Corbis, 58t Brand X Pictures/Jupiter
Images, 58b Larry Mulvehill/Corbis, 60 Brand X Pictures/Jupiter Images, 61 Digital Vision/Getty Images, 63 Flat Earth,
128/129 Brand X Pictures/Jupiter Images, 66/67 Image Ideas/Index Stock Imagery, Inc., 68 Digital Vision/Getty Images,
69 Image Ideas/Index Stock Imagery, Inc., 70 Brand X Pictures/Jupiter Images, 73 Photodisc/Getty Images, 74/75 Warren
Jacobi/Corbis, 76 Photodisc/Getty Images, 78 Photodisc/Getty Images, 79l Photodisc/Getty Images, 79m Photodisc/
Getty Images, 79r Photodisc/Getty Images, 81 NASA, 82 NASA, 84 NASA, 85t Photodisc/Getty Images, 86 NASA, 87
Photodisc/Getty Images, 88/89 NASA, 110/111 NASA